Earning Your Living
from Home

Patricia O'Reilly

Marino

Every effort has been made to ensure the accuracy of the information contained in this book at the time of going to press but provisions, regulations and legislation may subsequently change.

First published in 1996 by
Marino Books
An imprint of Mercier Press
16 Hume Street Dublin 2

Trade enquiries to Mercier Press
PO Box 5, 5 French Church
Street, Cork

© Patricia O'Reilly 1996

ISBN 1 86023 101 5

10 9 8 7 6 5 4 3 2 1

A CIP record for this title is
available from the British Library

Cover design by Adrienne
Geoghegan
Set by Richard Parfrey
Printed in Ireland by
ColourBooks, Baldoyle Industrial
Estate, Dublin 13

This book is dedicated to Susanne, who says she never will...

Contents

Foreword

Some of the great businesses of the world started on the kitchen table.

When my wife, Veronica, and I began to provide catering services from our home in 1967, we never dreamt that it would lead to a business which now employs over 2,000 people, and turns over £60 million.

Yet I still remember those difficult early days, when the business was run from home, and when we encountered many setbacks, brought on mainly by our own lack of knowledge and experience. How much easier it could have been had we avoided many of the basic pitfalls encountered by virtually every venture. Entering markets without sufficient research, picking the wrong people, lack of cost control and basic accounting information, inexpedient partnership arrangements, ineffective negotiating tactics, and failure to recognise the importance of existing customers were just some of the mistakes from which we first had to recover, and then to learn.

Experience is undoubtedly the greatest teacher, but all too often it proves to be too expensive. This book by Patricia O'Reilly provides a wealth of knowledge and experience from which today's home-based entrepeneurs can short-circuit this critical learning curve. I wish I could have read it back in 1967, and I wish you the success you deserve for taking the trouble to explore these pages.

Patrick Campbell
Chairman and Chief Executive
Campbell Bewley Group

1

Before You Begin

Each year in Ireland more and more people join the ranks of the thousands already earning their living from home, many doing so successfully. For some it is a dream come true, for others an option, for more a necessity. But if you've the right attitude, skills and a smattering of luck, everyone can do it.

For *Earning your Living from Home*, we have profiled, in Part II, a broad spectrum of people of varying age, gender, education, ability, location and financial circumstances. Their only common denominator is that they all earn their living from home. In our profiles we have tried to avoid the obvious and go for the more unusual.

These include the County Meath farmer who brought ostriches to Ireland; the marketing/PR director whose product achieved EC status; the Kerry family taking tourism by the horns; the couple running a health centre in Westport; the architect designing bird houses; the graduate who set up an electronic shopping mall; the potter who uses clay remedially; and the Castlebar-based teleworker with worldwide clients.

What Type of Business?

There is no easy way to identify suitable business opportunities. In times of recession, high unemployment and redundancies, the task is even more difficult with everyone fighting for a share of a declining market.

One rule of thumb that a successful importer applies is to go for a product that the majority, rather than the minority, of people require and where there's a gap in the market. You're elected if you come up with a commodity or service that hasn't been thought of before and which'll have the masses clamouring for it. If you've achieved that, you're hardly reading this!

People starting up a business on their own are usually either product or service orientated.

The range of products available is enormous. Walk around any supermarket, see the thousands that are shelved and think that each one started as an idea, some as the core idea, others as refinements on the original one.

Think of the vast and expanding arena of services that now exists. Up to a few years ago services such as car valeting, garden landscaping, window cleaning or ironing were rare in Ireland; now they're readily available.

The majority of people who operate their own businesses, and entrepreneurs in general, are passionate about what they do. When that passion is tempered with business acumen and the right type of personality, the sky's the limit.

The following is a list of just some of the areas open to the home earner, all of which can at least be administered from home:

Accountancy/Book-keeping, Antiques, Architecture, B and B, Beauty (facials, hairdressing, manicure, various treatments), Carpentry, Child Minding, Chiropody, Cleaning (houses/offices/windows), Complementary Medicine (aromatherapy, ki-massage, reflexology, etc.), Computing (desktop publishing, graphic design, software design, word processing), Conference Organisation, Consultancy, Cookery, Counselling, Curtain and Blind Making, Demonstrating, Dentistry, Doll and Teddy Bear Making, Dressmaking, Editing, Event Management, Farming (cattle, crops, dairy/deer/ostrich/ poultry), Giving Grinds, Handyman skills (decorating, plumbing, gardening), Horse Riding, Ironing, Indexing, Journalism, Kennelling, Law, Mail Order, Market Research, Medicine, Modelling, Property Development, Philately, Photography, Renting, Telemarketing/Telesales, Upholstering, Vehicle Servicing, Writing.

Thinking it Through

Many people wonder when is the best time to set up. Should they start the new year with a bang and make it the first of January? Perhaps spring, traditionally a time of new beginnings, or maybe September, the beginning of the academic year? It doesn't matter; earning your living from home is not seasonal.

As far back as Patrick Campbell can remember he wanted to own his own company. He began his business when the time was right for him. Today he is chairman of the Campbell Bewley Group. His philosophy in life has always been to do the common things uncommonly well. Campbell Catering was founded in 1967 by Patrick and his wife Veronica as a small firm supplying outdoor events. They then graduated to making sandwiches for Dublin schools and the rest, as they say, is history.

You must know what you want to do and can do. After realistically assessing your assets and liabilities, are you still determined to go ahead? Have you or can you raise start up capital?

Nothing in this world is as powerful as an idea whose time has come. When your time has come, you will begin.

Knowing what you want to do, being able to do it and being passionate about it is half the battle. In her autobiography, *Body and Soul*, Anita Roddick, founder of The Body Shop empire, says: 'To succeed you have to believe in something with such a passion that it becomes a reality.' But no matter how passionate you are about an idea there is not much point in setting up to trade as a philatelist if you don't know the first thing about stamps!

A hobby which has, say, made you an expert cabinet-maker, researcher or dressmaker can be the start of a business, especially if you've already begun to make money. You have the beginning of a client list and some idea of the potential markets when you decide positively to set about earning your living from it.

When you look for a loan you'll have more credibility and inspire more confidence if you're actually trading. It's a big jump from moonlighting to making a living, and selling a hobby item to a few friends and relatives may not necessarily be a realistic indication of the general public's attitude or the economic viability of your idea.

This book is about earning sufficient money to keep you and yours to whatever standard you aspire, rather than making pocket money from a hobby.

We will be looking at people, like Joan Hanna, founder of Craft T-Bear, who had a belief and who created and indeed, in some cases, cracked markets by their innovation and determination. Against all advice Joan was firmly convinced an international market existed for collectors' bears and how right she was.

Freelance journalist Patrick Quilligan, on the other hand, jumped in to fill a gap in the market with an import substitute and is committed to developing his mobile computer station, although he does not yet make his living exclusively from sales.

Assessing Your Assets and Liabilities

Basically the world can be divided into three types of people – those who make things happen, those who watch things happen and those who wonder what happened. If you're going to earn your living from home, it'll be easier for you if you fall into the 'those who make things happen' category.

While passion and enthusiasm are essential attributes, equally important is realistic assessment. You must be able to sit down and analyse your strengths and weaknesses, work out what skills you have, how best they can be put to use and then look objectively about how you could turn some of your weaknesses to strengths by taking, for example, a course in basic keyboarding or preliminary accountancy.

Before architect Simone Stephenson started The Birdhouse Company, she took a FÁS Business Appraisal Course, followed up with an Enterprise Development Programme. (She also received Forbairt funding for a feasibility study.)

Tapestry artist Angela Forte says the Craft Council's Business Training course was an invaluable foundation for her. 'When I finished college I hadn't a clue about the business end of crafts – the administration, accountancy or how to run a studio.'

Making your living is not something to be left to chance. Doing a bit of analysis and applying scientific techniques will maximise your chance of success. You need to be realistically aware of your pluses and minuses and to be able to apply them to your proposed project.

One approach that's used fruitfully in companies is brainstorming sessions. With friends and/or family, list out your training, leisure and business activities, specialist knowledge, experience and opposite each item make out a suitable business idea. Don't rule out even the seemingly ludicrous. It's amazing how often after a few days subconscious brewing such a thought can become the trigger for a practical idea.

If you're still unsure, can't make up your mind what you want to do, have no talents that scream out for recognition but really want to have a home-based income, settle down with a big jotter, a pencil and a rubber. List all your skills. Some of the questions you could ask yourself at this stage are:

- Can I type?
- Do I have a good command of English?
- Am I an accurate speller?
- Am I grammatically literate?
- Do I have the basics of accountancy?

If you've replied in the affirmative, you have the rudiments of business organisation. Think:

- What other things can I do?
- Do I enjoy doing them?
- What do I consider I'm most skilful at?
- Could I spend day after day, week after week, month after month, year after year doing it?

When you've isolated a skill/talent, next ask yourself:

- Is it commercially viable?
- Could I manage it?
- Is there an existing market niche for it?

If you've answered 'yes' to the above, check:

- Do I have all the necessary skills?
- If not, am I willing to acquire them?
- Is my home a suitable location to operate from?
- If not, can it be made so?
- Have I the necessary equipment?
- If not, can I acquire it?

Do your family call you mulish? Have you ever been told you're stubborn? Are you a self-starter? Are you determined to finish what you start? Do you have more determination, grit, sticking power, energy and commitment than the remainder of your friends? Are you prepared to overcome obstacles in the face of setbacks? Chances are if you've answered 'yes' to these questions, you're correctly motivated.

Do you have a nestegg that can be used to fund your project and to keep you in staples until the money starts coming in?

If not, have you enough financial credibility to get a loan?

Most businesses need some seed capital. If you've no way of acquiring it, you would want to think again about the feasibility of trying to earn your living from home.

In the majority of start up situations and even more so when operating from home, you, as the owner, are the business and will have to play many parts, make many key decisions without expert advice, depend on your own judgement and generally be the only driving force. Have you got what it takes? Read on.

2

Have You Got What It Takes?

From recent research it has emerged that certain characteristics are shared by people who set up in business alone.
These include:

- self-confidence
- persistence
- determination
- capability to set objectives
- drive and energy to implement objectives
- ability to live with uncertainty

Not everyone who successfully earns their living from home
possesses all these characteristics in equal measure. So don't
be put off if you aren't perfect! The acquisition of these traits
can be worked on. But one ingredient successful self-
employers, who include home earners, all have is common
sense. When you think of it, common sense is instinct;
enough of it is genius.

Paul's Story

Paul P. has many of the requisite entrepreneurial characteristics. He also had knowledge and experience and was willing
to take the risk.

He says his life began when he was made redundant. An
accomplished DIY-er, for years he had nurtured a dream of
refurbishing property commercially. 'I couldn't bring myself
to walk away from a guaranteed pay cheque at the end of
each month, over a month's holidays, sickness benefit and
a pension,' he says.

'But I decided to grasp this opportunity for all it was
worth and I didn't even look for another salaried job.'

He used part of his lump sum and borrowed the
remainder from the bank to buy a red brick terraced house,
which he planned to refurbish and sell. 'It's just as well I
didn't know what I was taking on,' he says. 'It was a
nightmare – it had to be re-wired, re-plumbed, central heating
fitted, new windows installed, roof repaired, re-plastered.
Some of the floor boards were rotten; several doors were
damaged beyond repair.'

To keep costs down he did most of the work himself, only
employing where necessary. It was an exhausting, frustrating,
exhilarating project that took over a year. He says he often
sat, looked and wondered would it ever be finished.
Eventually it was. He went for a letting rather than his
original plan of selling. Now on his third house, he regards
his first as an invaluable learning experience.

Characteristics of the Self-Employed

Take a look at the following:

• **Risk Taking**

From the outset you must realise that all business involves risk. What you may not know is that the majority of successful entrepreneurs go for moderate rather than large risks. Also, they know when to admit defeat on a project, cut their losses, get out and move on.

• **Dealing with Failure**

Remember it's how you handle failure, not whether you've been on the receiving end, that's important. It's OK to fail, but the successful entrepreneur learns from a setback and is willing to try again. If you're afraid of failure, you'll be afraid to take a risk.

• **Self-Confidence**

The type of self-confidence required for business is about being self-reliant and trusting your own ability when the going gets tough. But a bit of luck helps too!

• **Persistence and Determination**

Persistence, determination and the ability to overcome hurdles, solve problems and complete the job no matter what are vital.

- **Setting Objectives**

Successful business people set clear objectives and achieve them.

- **Initiative and Responsibility**

Initiative and responsibility are characteristics of success.

- **Using Resources and Services**

While self-reliance is important and admirable, it should not be at the expense of other services or advice on offer.

- **Living with Uncertainty**

As pointed out, business involves risk and takes time to establish, so you must be able to live with uncertainty and to commit to a project which may wear you to a frazzle, but not bear fruit for several years.

- **Drive and Energy**

You need a lot of drive and energy, the ability to work long hours and to function with less sleep than the majority of salaried workers.

- **Health**

Will your health stand up to the additional stress and longer working hours that come with being self-employed?

- **Business Acumen**

Sounds frightening. And it is if you haven't got it. In a nutshell, do you have a flair for business?

- **Experience**

What experience do you have? What skills do you need for the business you're going into? Can you and are you willing to acquire them?

Once you have drawn up a list of business ideas and done the personal analysis bit, the next step is to screen your ideas and draw up a shortlist, taking into account your own background and suitability. A recent survey carried out by the Bank of Ireland shows that a large number of successful start up businesses are closely associated with their owners' own business experience, leisure activity or training.

Tom Kehoe is one of the 2,500 – and growing – beekeeping enthusiasts in Ireland. His interest started as a hobby but has become his living. It all began when he joined his local beekeeping association. After a while he realised there was an opening for the retail supply of hives, protective clothing, hive smokers and all the other paraphernalia of beekeeping. His venture has been a success. He lives and trades at 106 North Circular Road, Dublin 7.

Chartered accountant Brian Gubbins, attracted by BES funding, saw the long-term potential to set up a family business in tourism when he bought Dunkerron House and self-catering cottages in Kenmare. These he used as both home and jump off point for the family entrée into Rent-an-Irish Cottage.

Brian Purcell farmed cattle for years. It was while he was travelling in South Africa that he came up with the idea of starting ostrich farming in Ireland. He plans with grant aid to set up the first ostrich abattoir in Ireland.

The background and training of Don and Jo Maher, founders of Boyton Catering, are firmly rooted in the hotel/catering industry. They had the training, experience and ability to realise and to implement their idea.

Good business ideas don't just happen; they are achieved by detailed research and constant searching. Frequently worthwhile ideas are stumbled on while pursuing other business or leisure interests.

Next let's take a realistic look at the pluses and minuses of earning your living from home.

3

The Pluses and Minuses

Favourable Climate

Small business has been a growth industry in Ireland for the past two decades. Currently some 98 per cent of the country's estimated 160,000 non-farm businesses are small within business/banking definition, i.e. under 50 employees, with under £3 million in annual turnover.

Yes, I realise this book is about earning your living from home; that we're not talking about employee numbers and that you'd probably make the *Guinness Book of Records* working from home with such numbers and turnover.

The point is that the economic climate is right, technology is favourable and as a people we're comfortable with the small business syndrome.

In international circles we're regarded as a nation of micro-businesses, because more than 90 per cent of our enterprises employ fewer than ten people. In total, small business accounts for half of all employment in the private sector.

Many entrepreneurs are succeeding in working from home, though few realised at the start just what they were letting themselves in for, but the consensus of opinion is that when you've the business up and running it is worth the sleepless nights, the nail chewing worry, the long hours, lack of leisure and reduced financial circumstances to be your own boss and even better to be working from home.

For architect couple Tony and Geraldine O'Daly the bonuses of operating from home far outweigh the disadvantages. Adaptable hours allow Tony to work in the evenings, which he favours, and Geraldine operates on flexi-time. As domestic work makes up a large percentage of their portfolio, they're available for clients after hours. They like being on tap for the children, reckon they've heightened family life and even take the occasional day off.

Equally, Jill Aston owner of Cake Craft says the main benefits for her of working from home are being there for her children, not having to pay childcare and being able to choose her working hours – which, she says, often don't start until about nine o'clock at night.

Origins of Homeworking

Homeworking is long established – it has been on the go in Ireland since Brehon times when we were a matriarchal society with a powerful breed of woman having it all, as we'd say today.

In Dublin's Liberties at the end of the eighteenth century some 25,000 people were employed in weaving, whole families operating from home, the majority descended from the Huguenots who had come to Ireland in the 1600s. Then with the advent of industry and the mushrooming of factories, working from home lost favour.

Teleworking

In recent years working at home has grown again in popularity, one impetus being the opportunities offered by teleworking. Teleworking is a growth industry with an ever-increasing demand for skilled workers, as Regina McGarrigle, owner of Mayo Editorial Services confirms. 'When I decided to work full-time, I discovered there was great demand for qualified freelance editors and I had no problem lining up clients.'

Teleworking is ideal for the self-employed and perfect for operating from home. For the more gregarious, telecottaging, local centres equipped with modern technology where a group of people work, is another viable option.

Under the generic term 'teleworking' is included the increasingly successful telemarketing. Telemarketing is the systematic use of a telephone as a communications channel between an organisation and its customers.

An indication of the growth in telemarketing in Ireland is the annual increase in the usage of the Freefone 1800 Service. Since its introduction in 1990, the service grew by the end of March 1994 to 7.2 million calls.

The term telemarketing is being constantly updated and many firms now refer to this type of activity as 'telebusiness' or 'teleservicing'. The main reason for Ireland's telemarketing success is that it's a proven cost effective communication channel, time management effective and, where appropriate, an effective sales channel. An increasing number of businesses are using home-based telemarketing operatives.

Other successful teleworking operations being carried out from a home or a telecottage base range from distance learning, writing, editing, graphic design, illustration, to compilation of aviation manuals, management consultancy, computer and business skills, training and translations.

Statistics

To date there are no official figures for the numbers of people in Ireland earning their living from home, but there is no reason to suppose our statistics vary much from Britain where about 5 per cent of the working population work mainly from home or live at their place of work.

According to the Henly Centre for Forecasting, more than 50 per cent of self-employed people and 25 per cent of full-time employees are currently working from home at least some of the time. By the year 2000 it is estimated that the number of full-time employees working at home will have risen to around a third.

Data from the 1991 UK Census suggests that the gender differences in working at home are not great, though men working from home do outnumber women. This is partly explained by the fact that the broad definition of home working includes agricultural workers, farmers and those 'living above the shop'.

Higher socio-economic groups are more likely to work from home according to the data. Only 1.9 per cent of unskilled manual workers reported that they worked at home. These figures are in marked contrast to employers and managers of whom 7.8 per cent said they worked at home or from home. Another unsurprising fact to emerge is that highly qualified men earn significantly more than highly qualified women in the same field.

Homeworking *vs.* Commuting

The good news for both sexes is that, according to a recent survey carried out by British Telecom, homeworkers are 45 per cent less likely to become ill than commuters.

It was an Englishman who invented commuting in 1829. George Shillibeer set up the first horse-drawn London 'bus' service which ran daily from a pub in Paddington to the Bank. Figures in 1995 show that daily, one million people commute to London. But it wasn't until the 1880s and then in the States that the word 'commuter' became popular – a commuter being somebody who bought a commutation ticket (season ticket).

Think of the joys of never having to commute again. No more battling with traffic to crawl to work; no more rooting for parking spaces; no more waiting for buses; no more taking your life in your hands pedalling through rush hour; no more pavement jostling; no more desperate taxis. All that's gone once you operate out of your home.

A further survey carried out for British Telecom claims that homeworkers are generally fitter and healthier than their office colleagues. They suffer from fewer colds and headaches (even fewer toothaches), take less time off sick and get approximately 45 per cent more work done.

The main source of working stress, according to this survey, is commuting. Stress can lead to physical ailments such as headaches, migraines, high blood-pressure and heart disease, and is one of the biggest killers in the world. Traffic and industrial pollution increase the risk of asthma, bronchitis and other illnesses and public transport along with the office environment allows the transmission of a variety of bugs.

As well as reducing stress levels, risk of infection and the likelihood of being involved in one of the 35,000 commuter car accidents a year in the UK, less time spent travelling means more time for relaxation and leisure activities which boost physical and emotional wellbeing. All of which, the survey concludes, makes giving up going out to work sound as positive a health move as giving up smoking.

But working from home, particularly if you're a teleworker, can have health drawbacks, claims Professor David Oborne, a psychologist at the University of Wales. He recently completed a three-year study into the psychological and organisational aspects of teleworking and says that working at home can lead to loneliness and the loss of creative impetus, causing depression, anxiety and stress.

Regina McGarrigle does not agree with these findings. She says the very nature of teleworking requires a quiet interruption-free environment. But Tony O'Connell who operates Channel-One, an electronic shopping mall, from his home, confesses to feelings of isolation. His solution? The purchase of a guinea pig which he called Elvis.

One of the reasons pinpointed by Professor Oborne is that the blurring of the traditional work/home boundaries can lead to tension that could effect the physical and emotional health of the family. Working at home cuts us off from the emotional support that organisations provide. Most of us need feedback, but something we'd ask somebody sitting at the next desk we might consider too trivial to make a phone call about. The boss, in passing, may comment on our good work but is less likely to ring home to tell us.

Direct physical injury is another risk. We're less likely to use ergonomically designed equipment at home and more likely to work in cramped or poorly lit conditions. Added to this, technology can be addictive and without correct supervision it can lead to complaints such as headaches, impaired vision, backache and repetitive strain injury (RSI).

Still with us? Next let's check out the courses that are available for the budding home-based entrepreneur.

4

Which Courses?

It's well worth taking a look at the various courses on offer.
While this chapter is primarily devoted to existing courses
from the Crafts Council of Ireland, FÁS and the Project
Development Centre, all of whose main purpose is to give
the embryo self-employed entrepreneur a foundation in the
business of running a business, do keep your ear to the
ground locally for the acquisition of additional skills. The
courses on offer by the Vocational Educational Committee
(VEC) and its city of Dublin counterpart, CDVEC, are
particularly worth looking into. Here it has to be said that
by and large courses are geared towards manufacturing
rather than service industries.

Crafts Council of Ireland

Craft and Design Business Development Course

The purpose of this forty-two-week Kilkenny-based course
is to equip craftspeople and designers/makers with the
necessary skills to set up as entrepreneurs, with the potential

to create further employment in their business. In keeping with the Crafts Council's mission the business, as well as being commercially viable, must also contribute to improved standards in contemporary Irish design and craft production.

There are no fees for EU citizens; participants receive £70 per week and, on successful completion, Crafts Council certification. Over 70 per cent of people who completed the course over the past five years now run their own businesses and many are employers.

Acceptance for the course requires a clear concept of the range of products/designs to be marketed and the technical capacity for commercial production. Applicants are selected by portfolio interview. While the objective of the interview is to assess creative ideas and production skills, the business proposals are equally important. Applicants should know their markets, who their competitors are, where to source material and what type of equipment is required for production.

The course includes:

- development of designs
- product development
- prototype
- product promotion
- design quality
- production efficiency
- market research on pricing and retail structure
- sales techniques
- preparation of business plans
- accounting

Each course member is allocated a mentor from their own production/design discipline. The acid test for product development is the sales of work produced – Christmas sales in the Council's gallery in Dublin and the 'Showcase' trade fair in January.

FÁS

Through its training centre network, FÁS provides close on 170 different training courses of industrial and commercial nature. Courses range from Accounting, Alarm Installation, Beautician, various aspects of Computers, Data/Telecommunications, Engineering, Food Technology, Graphics and Desktop Publishing to Office Procedures, Quality Control, Robot Technology and Control, Video Production and Welding.

The courses are designed to equip participants with specific skills to enhance their employment prospects through training. Courses are available to men and women who are unemployed, redundant, out of full-time education, those wishing to update their skills or to change their careers and for school leavers unable to obtain employment. Applicants who must register with their local FÁS Employment Services Offices are interviewed to determine the training best suited to their needs.

Course costs are borne by FÁS. Trainees receive allowances, subsidised accommodation costs, if necessary, and subsidised transport for those who have to travel three miles or more from residence to training.

FÁS Business Appraisal Training Programme

The aim of this ten-week course is to provide people who have a business idea with the necessary skills to assess its viability with the objective of becoming self-employed. Recruitment is by interview and is open to anyone with a business idea and a commitment to becoming self-employed. Successful programme participants receive FÁS/City and Guilds Introductory Enterprise Skills Certificate.

Enterprise payments may be available to support participants' incomes – £40 per week for self-employed people without dependants; £65 per week for those with dependants. The conditions for receiving these payments include:

- Being unemployed, signing on the live register, receiving Unemployment Assistance, Unemployment Benefit or Disability Benefit for thirteen weeks immediately beforehand.
- Business proposed must be potentially viable, full-time and independent, comply with relevant legislation and not displace other businesses.
- Capital spending must not exceed £30,000 in first year of trading and cannot be in certain areas of activity, such as gaming.
- Business must not commence before FÁS approval is received.

Course contents include:

- market research/planning
- selling techniques
- business plans
- insurance/legal aspects
- financial/research/planning
- book-keeping/taxation
- new technology

The Project Development Centre

Enterprise Development Programme

The Project Development Centre, an initiative of the Dublin Institute of Technology, was founded in 1983 to assist young Irish graduate entrepreneurs in the areas of innovation, product development and enterprise creation.

The aim of this programme is to facilitate graduate entrepreneurs to develop the skills and expertise to establish and run their own businesses. It is a full-time, fifty-two week interactive course, focusing on the individual business, with hands-on development integrated with strategic workshops, training modules, group participation and feedback.

The main thrust of the course is on business planning and the actual development of the business. Generally there are two programmes annually – one commencing in January and one in July. Applications are invited two months in advance.

Support

- financial, funded through the European Social Fund – each participant is eligible for a grant allowance of £85 per week
- training, workshops and training modules to examine the key elements of the business
- mentor, assigned to each participant to help in business development, exploring ideas, formulating plans, directing and counselling

Projects

- knowledge-based
- innovative
- job creation potential
- export potential
- manufacturing or service areas

(The proposed business should be well researched prior to application)

Participants

- open to graduates of all third level colleges
- policy is to fund graduates under the age of thirty-five
- potential entrepreneurial skills required
- projects with team involvement welcomed

Application

Application takes the form of a short business proposal, two to three pages in length, which should sell the concept to the programme management.

It should contain:

- an outline of the business
- the potential of the business
- objectives and targets
- reasons for applying to the programme

A current CV should also be included.

Vocational Education Committee (VEC)

As well as the above courses, it's worth looking at the 250 plus PLC (Post Leaving Certificate) courses on offer from the Vocational Education Committees (VEC) throughout the country. Call into your local college for information.

The majority of students taking these courses have done the Leaving Certificate; course acceptance can involve an interview. The VEC provides its own certification and additional certification for specific courses has been obtained from selected outside examining and professional bodies.

Many of the courses on offer are suitable for people earning their living from home or as an additional skill. They include Accounting, Administration, Advertising, Business Studies, Catering, Child Care, Communications, Computer Applications, Craft, Computer Aided Design, Computer Programming, Furniture Restoration, Horticulture, Interior Design, Journalism, Layout, Marketing, Montessori, Public Relations, Scriptwriting for TV and Radio, Start Your Own Business, Tax and Word Processing.

Next, we're looking at the mechanics of start up.

5

The Mechanics of Start up

Space

Obviously your type of business dictates the kind of space and equipment required.

What we're concerned about in this chapter is the office-type scenario without which most businesses won't survive. For the administrative end of your business – and I haven't yet come across a business that doesn't require some form of administration – ideally you need space for a desk, a chair, filing cabinet, word processor. And it's a bonus to have a phone at your elbow. An answering machine is almost mandatory unless you're going to get a mobile phone and then there's the handiness of a fax, especially one that also photocopies.

In theory acquiring the space for this sounds simple, but when you come down to practicalities, it can be difficult, as with modern living it's often hard to find even a quiet corner, much less a room in many homes. If the ideal space isn't available when you're starting out, don't be put off, make do. Many businesses that start at home have to be moved to outside premises once they become successful.

One of the most important aspects to running any business is efficient paperwork kept up to date and to achieve this you don't need a state-of-the-art office – though it would be nice!

An accountant, dealing in small accounts and operating from home keeps the out-of-date paperwork from his clients' accounts in a suitcase. Current accounts are kept in a cardboard box and he works out of the dining-room, also used by his wife for her counselling sessions, where she has appropriated for her notes a drawer that locks in an antique cabinet.

The ideal scenario is a room preferably on the ground floor that can be turned into an office, so that if you have clients calling you can see them without having them trailing upstairs, should your office be a converted bedroom.

A well-known Dublin-based PR executive operates in great style with regularly updated decor out of a converted garage with an enormous bay window looking out into the garden. Initially the idea of this was resisted fiercely by her husband who claimed the space, not for his car, but for mementoes dating back to his childhood, which were reduced to manageable numbers and are now happily housed in the attic.

She designed the space and acquired the equipment to specifically meet her requirements. As well as a computer, she has a photocopier (necessary for press releases), a franking machine (she passionately hates licking stamps), and a fax on a separate line to her telephone. The space is designed so that shelves within reach of the desk accommodate reference books; easy chairs and low table are angled to maximise the garden view; and fresh coffee perks all day.

Equipment

Equipment such as desk, chair and filing cabinet can be picked up secondhand, as viewing alone is adequate. But computer, fax and telephone answering machine can be more difficult. The golden rule is that unless you're sure of the source, can try out or get a guarantee, buy new. For stationery, headed notepaper, business cards, compliment slips, shop around local printers.

Computer

The justification for getting a computer is to increase the efficiency of your business at least enough to offset its cost. To assess your needs, start by making a list of all the areas in which a computer could be used in your business – standard letters and circulars, costings, estimates and quotations, book-keeping and preparation of accounts, invoices and statements, financial projections (including forecasting of cashflow and profit and loss). If a lot of your time is taken up in these areas, a computer would be of benefit.

The best sources of information on computers are:

• friends who work with computers
• somebody in your line of business

- computer courses, ranging from the brief to the advanced
- computer exhibitions
- computer magazines

You'll most likely be looking for a personal computer (PC or Apple Mac). This is one stage up from a home computer, and one stage down from a mini-computer (a misnomer for a powerful machine with several terminals). A computer correctly used will be of assistance to almost any business and is likely very quickly to justify itself either in financial or time-saving terms.

At first glance, the personal computer market is a bewildering one. There are dozens of brand names and scores of variants, all extolling their own technical virtues.

Take your time choosing both your computer hardware and software. Improvements are made every few months so no matter what equipment you buy it'll be technically out of date by the time it reaches your desk. Once you've a computer, the door is open for you to use it more ways than you would have originally intended. The installation of a modem allows you to transmit copy via the phone.

Laptops or notebooks, as they're now more commonly called, are becoming increasingly popular. And the good news is that almost as fast as they're improving, their price is coming down. They're totally portable, the heaviest weighing no more than 9 lbs, sturdy, with about 9.5 inch screens, either colour (more expensive) or black and white, and with finger-friendly keyboards. They operate off mains or a re-chargeable battery which gives you a good three to four hours computing time before having to plug in. For a small business operation, they're ideal. You can work on the train or plane, make notes at meetings and it's much more sociable to be able to sit with the family and key in rather than having to isolate yourself at your desk.

Computer software is all, and, particularly since the advent of Windows, becoming more sophisticated and more user-friendly by the minute. Most people's requirements are met with integrated packages which combine word processing, database, spreadsheet and communications functions.

Make sure the package you choose will fulfil your requirements. Shop around, as prices vary. If you're not familiar with computers, it's a good idea to talk to an expert, outlining your specific personal and/or business requirements.

If you need a day's training, get it sooner rather than later. But not so soon that you aren't casually familiar with your machine and its software, so that you can list your requirements. One point – make sure before signing up and paying that your specific requirements will be met. Many of these courses are secretary- rather than owner-orientated.

Desk and Chair

If you've your own space, get your own desk and chair, making sure, if at all possible, that they are ergonomically sound. You can pick up a second hand desk quite cheaply – if you're lucky, even an antique model.

A root around the auction rooms, your local office suppliers whose clients often trade up by trading in, scanning the papers or a browse through the twice-weekly *Buy and Sell* should be successful. Or how about a mobile computer work station? There is a profile of Patrick Quilligan, who conceived, designed and implemented one, in Part II.

Your chair can range from a cast off kitchen model – inexpensive, but not recommended – to the latest, adjustable to your size and shape – highly applauded, but expensive. For a price range in between, try the same sources as for a desk.

Fax

With instant communication and, indeed, escalating telephone charges, the facsimile or fax, as it is more colloquially known, is fast becoming another popular piece of equipment. It allows exact duplicates of documents whether handwritten, line-drawn or typed to be transmitted over the telephone lines. Before buying, make sure that the usage justifies the cost.

Filing Cabinet

In these high-tech days, even the idea of a filing cabinet can be the personification of the mundane, but think – have you ever seen a successful business without at least one? If you're starting off, you don't have to buy a spanking new model; the same sources cited for desk and chair should prove successful.

Telephone Answering Machine

This has become an invaluable piece of everyday equipment, increasingly in the home as well as the office. The kind that allows you pick up your messages while away from your workplace is the most efficient. Such a machine has the benefits of a mobile phone, in that you are never too long out of contact, but it does allow you control of returning calls, is much less intrusive and also less expensive than a mobile.

Stationery

If you've a high profile business where presentation is important, it's worth getting printed good quality headed notepaper, business cards and compliment slips. They reflect you and your business.

Get prices from three printers, making sure to check paper quality. Pro rata it's more economical to buy 2,000 rather than 100, but if you're getting all three from the same source, you should be able to negotiate at least a 10 per cent discount. Buy boxes of envelopes, computer paper, etc., from your local office supplier – better value than from local newsagent type shops.

Before going any further let's spend some time on testing your market.

6

Testing Your Market

This chapter is entitled 'Testing Your Market', rather than 'Marketing', because the word 'Marketing' can be a turn-off. But it shouldn't be. Marketing is mostly common sense. International business guru Peter Druker maintains that marketing is so basic that it cannot exist separately. It is the whole business seen from the point of view of its final result, that is, from the customer's point of view. In layman's terms this means that to be a bullfighter you must first learn to be a bull.

Marie Cooney, Marketing/PR director of Tipperary Natural Mineral Water, recognises that marketing is the life-blood of her business. Initially it was a case of recognising, grasping and manoeuvering every opportunity with a product she believed in and using every PR opportunity to ensure its high profile. It has worked.

Even if your business has adequate backing and does get off the ground, the enterprise does not end there. Once you get started you've to build on foundations strong enough to secure survival. Many great ideas get off to a kick start, but fall by the wayside because of blinkered thinking.

The most widely accepted definition of marketing is: 'Satisfying customer needs at a profit'. The birth of marketing coincided with the upsurge in demand for consumer products which began in the late 1940s. It is only during the last ten years that marketing has emerged as a recognised and separate skill in Ireland. Up to then marketing and selling were regarded as interchangeable. Even today many people have difficulty defining marketing and visualising the activities it involves.

Marketing deals not only with goods and services, but also with ideas. It covers everything from research, product planning and development to promotion and, of course selling. Selling is the process of negotiating and carrying out that transaction.

Traditionally in Ireland we're guilty of employing a product-orientated selling philosophy, which means that we're inclined to focus attention on the product or service, rather than on its selling and marketing.

This is a trap that is very easy for those of you working from or considering working from home to fall into, because as we've said earlier many people earning their living from home have had the talent, the hobby, the idea before sussing out the market.

It has worked for many, particularly people of an artistic disposition, like tapestry artist Angela Forte who had the courage to take a gamble and go for the creative, rather than the commercial; Dave Dain whose career as a potter started with his fascination for it; painter Anne O'Shea whose first love is portraits and her partner Maurice Noble's enthusiasm for giant puppets.

But for the majority of us without specific artistic talent, finding a gap in the market and filling it is more likely to succeed in these consumer orientated times.

Market Research

Researching your market is nothing as formidable as it sounds. It just means making sure an opening exists for the product, idea or service you have in mind; or looking for a niche that you can fill.

If you're not sure of your market and you need to research it, you can do most of it yourself from readily available sources. Dubliners are lucky as the library in the Ilac Centre is such a useful source of information. However the majority of libraries in the various towns and cities have comprehensive reference sections where trade directories and publications relating to your proposed business may be referred to. The *Golden Pages* and telephone directories and official digests of statistics are other sources of information.

Depending on the business you're looking into, Further Facts in Part III should also provide you with information, as should your local Chamber of Commerce. Asking triggers information and most people will be only too willing to point you down the correct road.

If you've done some preliminary work you can always test your market with a dry run to get response at a local level. Never underestimate the power of making a local foray before going nationally and then, hopefully, internationally! The local market can be sussed out for a small outlay, perhaps by distributing some leaflets (rope your own or neighbours' children in for the legwork); or putting cards on shop noticeboards (the ones in supermarkets attract a good response). Space out distribution in case you're so overwhelmed by response that you'll have difficulty filling orders!

A large part of market research is knowing your competitors. The *Golden Pages* or one of the many local directories distributed to householders will give you a list of similar businesses in your area or nationally. Familiarise yourself with their products.

Just as an example, let's suppose that you're manufacturing leprechauns. In what way do yours differ from your competitors? List the pluses and minuses. What's special about yours? What's special about theirs? Why should people prefer one to the other? What unique features have your competitors that you could incorporate (with due regard to infringement of copyright or patents)?

Send for relevant promotional literature and price lists, attend trade exhibitions. If your competitors sell through retail outlets, go and see their display and promotion at point of sale. Watch particularly for their publicity and advertising; for you to succeed, yours will have to be different and better.

Sales

With all due respects to Ralph Waldo Emerson (US essayist) he was mistaken – no matter how good your products, in this competitive, economically aware commercial climate the world will not beat a path to your home clamouring for them; you have to bring them to the world. However fabulous and original your leprechauns may be, if you do not seek out those garden aficionados, they will be left on your hands.

The time to start planning for sales is when your product or service is still on the drawing board. At this point nothing is lost if you find out that your idea, however good of its kind, will not command a large enough market to make a profit. Perhaps it will be so expensive to produce that its price will be prohibitive; or perhaps enough people won't buy green-jacketed leprechauns to make them commercially viable. Questions to ask yourself at the planning stage include:

- What exactly am I offering?
- Who will be my customers and where shall I find them?
- Who are my competitors and in what way is my product an improvement on theirs or a better alternative (leprechaun *vs.* stone swan!)?
- What is the best way of making my product or service known to the customer?
- When do I start planning for the future?

Now that we've handled some of the preliminaries of marketing, we'll wait until Chapter 14 to deal with selling. But for now, let's take a look at getting funding.

7

Getting Funding

'Business is other people's money,' maintained nineteenth-century French entrepreneur, Madame de Girardin, and it hasn't changed in the past 100 years.

Unless you have your own money or can rely on family, the majority of people starting up in business today think in terms of borrowing. While no business can function without money, it is possible to set up without external funding. Dhara Kelly and Emer Gaffney who own Cloona Health Centre in Westport did; so did Patrick Quilligan, Joan Hanna and also Don and Jo Maher of Boyton Catering.

If you're a viewer/listener/reader of advertisements, you're likely thinking, 'No problem. The financial institutions are out there queuing up to lend me money.' That's the theory – the practice can be much different and does require bureaucratic patience which Patrick Quilligan admits he doesn't have. So he started in a small way, waiting until his first lot of units sold before he started manufacturing again.

Banks

When we consider borrowing, the banks are usually the first institutions that come to mind. The best way is to make either a telephone query or call into your local branch to have a preliminary chat with the manager.

Before we get immersed in this chapter, did you know that overdrafts are in theory repayable on demand, and are always at a variable rate? This means that the borrower has less certainty than with a term loan which may be at a fixed rate? (More about term loans further on.)

First Impressions

A brief tip – first impressions have a 70 per cent impact. People who look successful inspire more confidence and are regarded as having a better chance of succeeding. So even if you're just dropping in on spec to make an appointment to see the manager, forget the jeans and favourite sweatshirt. Be groomed.

Anne R. planned to set up a crèche in her home. The project required a garage conversion, purchase of equipment and a bank loan in the region of £7,000. 'I handled the bank as though I was buying lamb chops. In I landed dressed in leggings, trainers and a T-shirt with no preparation,' she says. 'I learned my lesson. Since then I've always been businesslike about a business proposal.' The good news is that at the bank's suggestion she put together a business proposal and within a few weeks received the loan.

Credit Unions

Many people are unfamiliar with the facilities offered for small loans by credit unions. Credit unions started in Ireland in the late 1950s, a decade of depression, high unemployment and emigration. Credit unions are non-profit making financial co-operatives owned and controlled by members for members. Their philosophy is that they exist to service the financial needs of the community and to retain members' savings within the community for the benefit of members.

Credit unions consider loan applications from members for what they term: 'any worthwhile purpose' and would regard a viable proposition to earn a living from home as one. By law loan interest is charged at not more than 1 per cent per month on the reducing loan balance, representing an annual rate of 12.68 per cent. There are no fees or transaction charges. The best approach is to call into your local branch.

According to the credit union, the following are the advantages to borrowing from it:

- Loan application dealt with on its own merits.
- Repayments tailored to meet your personal circumstances.
- Your loan up to £15,000 will be insured at no direct cost to you. Under certain conditions, this cover can extend to £30,000.
- Interest payable only on reducing balance of loan.
- Repayment schedule adjusted to meet changing circumstance, if necessary.

County Enterprise Boards

Thirty-five County Enterprise Boards are located throughout the twenty-six counties of Ireland. They operate out of County Council offices and are managed at a national level by the Department of Enterprise and Employment. Their primary objective is to encourage the development of small and start up enterprises supporting local entrepreneurship and enterprise with the aim of building a strong local economy.

The Enterprise Fund assists through grant aid. Typical example of Enterprise Funding is Ciaran Ganter, who received a £5,000 grant and the support of a mentor to start Candlewood, his beeswax candlemaking enterprise.

The Fund supports:

* Individual, group or community projects providing products or services with the capacity to achieve commercial viability.
* Preparation of feasibility studies and business plans aimed at assessing the viability of projects.

The grant levels that apply are:

* A maximum of 50 per cent of the cost of capital and other investment or £50,000 – whichever is the lesser.
* A maximum of 75 per cent of the cost of preparing a feasibility study/business plan to an overall limit of £5,000 in the case of a single project.

- An employment grant of up to £5,000 per person subject to a maximum of £50,000 is also available. Fifty per cent of this is payable when employee commences employment, the remainder when job(s) have been in existence for six months.

Projects qualifying for assistance by the Enterprise Boards must be in the commercial sphere and regarded as capable of achieving economic viability. In particular there should be:

- a market for the proposed project or service
- availability of adequate overall finance
- appropriate managerial and technical capacity to implement the project.

First Step

First Step, established in 1991, provides interest-free start up loans and a business mentor for three years to projects which cannot access funding (or sufficient funding) from other sources. The money comes from a revolving fund provided by international corporations, national companies and The Ireland Fund.

It is spearheaded by Norma Smurfit, fundraising entrepreneur. By 1995 First Step had lent out in excess of £1.5m to some 300 projects, involving in the region of 600 jobs. Criteria are that the proposed project is commercially viable, thoroughly researched and presented with a business plan.

Activities supported by First Step include Brendan Lawless' BRS Designs, kitchen, bathroom and bedroom units. Like many an entrepreneur before him, without funding he would have been stymied. An opportunity to set up a showroom brought him to First Step, where he received a £12,000 loan.

Another First Step protégé is Clonmel-based Choices, who design and manufacture Irish dancing costumes. Set up in 1993, it was initially operated from home by sisters Breda Murray, Kathleen Blake and Margaret Browne. They came up with the idea when their own children became involved in Irish dancing.

Since the success of *Riverdance* triggered a universal public interest in Irish dancing, Choices' market has become increasingly international. In America, Australia, Germany and Holland, Irish dancing schools are blossoming; Irish dancers are crying out for authentic costumes, and are willing to pay upwards to £475 for a customised dress.

'From the beginning we had more orders than we could fill,' says Breda Murray. 'Our problem was not finding a market, rather it was properly funding Choices. We went to First Step, because we had difficulty raising funding locally.' Within a year they were employing eleven people, including FÁS trainees working towards their City and Guilds Certificate examinations. The sisters' projection is for fifty jobs in the short term. 'We want to bring all the elements under one roof and we're going to have to move to bigger premises,' says Breda Murray.

It is First Step policy, where possible, to match funds from, say, local county enterprise boards who grant aid machinery and equipment up to 50 per cent, the Ireland Fund in the border counties; and, where applicable, Údarás na Gaeltachta in Irish-speaking areas of the country. Some projects financed by First Step may be funded only to a maximum of 50 per cent of the start up costs and in such cases evidence of matching funds may be required. Personal and credit references are necessary.

Chapter 8 is about professionally drawing up your business plan.

8

Drawing Up Your Business Plan

The Business Plan

If you're looking for external financing, a business plan is probably the most important document you'll ever prepare. Simone Stephenson (bird houses), Tony O'Connell (electronic shopping mall), Ciaran Ganter (beeswax candles) and Angela Forte (tapestries) all agree.

In theory one of the main keys to successful business is planning your project properly from the beginning; in practice, while it is important to keep to a structure, it is equally important to recognise a viable opportunity and to go for it.

The discipline of having to compile a business plan when starting up is a vital exercise. It doesn't matter how small your business is, planning gives it structure, consolidates your purpose and gives you goals to aim towards. Your plan should be prepared on a realistic rather than a pessimistic or optimistic basis. Issues to be covered include management, marketing, operation and finance.

The purpose of preparing a business plan is to provide a detailed, logical but flexible framework on which to plan over a three- to five-year period. It acts as a base to assess and evaluate future performance. Most importantly it forms a basis for discussion on matters financial and is vital if you're looking for financing.

The business plan structure set out below is courtesy of AIB. Before you start reading, remember each plan is individual and the focus of yours will depend on your type of business.

Included in your business plan should be:

• **Introduction, Concise Summary and Overview**

• **Business Details**

    business name or trading name
    business address
    business telephone number
    business activities
    type of business
    date of commencement
    name and address of legal adviser
    name and address of accountant (if applicable)
    VAT registration number

- **Keyperson Details**

  name
  address
  telephone number
  date of birth
  qualifications
  work experience
  business experience
  courses attended
  existing bank accounts
  personal assets

- **Objectives**

  personal objectives
  business objectives
  (short, medium and long term evaluation and indication
  as to achievement)

- **Management**

  any additional skills required?

- **Marketing**

  describe your particular market
  who are your customers?
  is this market growing, static or in decline?
  list competition

- **Your Product or Service**

    what is special about it?
    what advantage?
    identify market niche
    if relevant, describe branding, design, packaging etc.

- **Selling**

    projected sales and market share
    pricing
    competitors' pricing
    terms of sale
    methods of selling/distribution
    customer base
    promotions and advertising strategy
    public relations strategy

- **Production**

    describe the production process
    cost and supply of raw materials
    machinery, equipment requirements

- **Finance**

    estimate costs of:
    equipment
    working capital

detail assumptions used for costings of:
sales revenue
cost of sales
administrative and selling expenses

detail proposed source of funds:
amount of investment by keyperson
other investment
what are your financing requirements from bank?
what assets are available as security?
describe your record-keeping system.

At this stage don't give up on your project. Yes, the whole idea is intimidating. But the above is a total business plan. For your business, it can be modified and adapted to meet your specific borrowing requirements. The main thing to bear in mind is that you must have a thorough understanding of your requirements and before you can get a loan you'll have to present them, clearly documented.

Whether you're borrowing to set up your business or using existing funds, money management including a knowlege of financial terminology is vital. Each year the majority of businesses, both large and small, go to the wall because the principals keep too loose an accounting control.

Cashflow

Cashflow simply means the cash that comes into your business and the cash that goes out. A cashflow projection is essential to determine your working capital – the day-to-day finance you need to keep your business going. It's important to make a realistic cashflow forecast as cashflow problems can be the death of many a new business. You need to be familiar with the meaning of terms such as profit and loss forecast.

Banking Facilities

- Overdraft – flexible financing facility for short term borrowing, such as seasonal cashflow fluctuations.
- Bridging finance – interim funding for business.
- Term loans – mainly used for purchasing medium to long term fixed assets or for medium term working capital.
- Loan accounts – for a longer term repayment schedule, or when repayment period is unclear.
- Instalment purchase – this facility can be used for a wide range of items, which become your property at the end of agreed term of fixed payments.
- Leasing – an attractive method of financing that involves no capital outlay. Ideal for acquiring equipment, especially when you need to conserve capital.
- Insurance premium finance – if you're required to take out insurance, with agreement your bank may pay the premium up front and set your payments on a fixed rate.
- Professional fees finance – often once-offs that can upset working capital and can be spread over fixed monthly instalments.

If you're operating from home and starting in a small way it is unlikely that you'll need all the above facilities, but it's a good policy to know as much as you can about all aspects of your business, especially the money end. It gives a feeling of security.

Now that you've sorted out your business plan, let's take a look at whether or not you should employ an accountant.

9

Should You Employ an Accountant?

Only you can decide whether or not you should employ an accountant. If you already know something about business accounting and revel in figures, you may be able to do without one. But bear in mind that however nimble you are with figures, you're unlikely to have an accountant's grasp of the innumerable regulations relating to taxation or an accountant's all-round familiarity with different aspects of business.

Tony Moore operates a consulting engineering business from home, servicing clients throughout Ireland. He firmly believes that ineffectual handling of financial matters is one of the major pitfalls for the self-employed, often contributing more than lack of actual work to failure. 'Not using an accountant or a book-keeper is the rock you can perish on,' he says. 'But rather than employ, negotiate a fee or a contract sum.'

If you're planning to set up a limited company, which we're looking at in the next chapter, an accountant is definitely recommended, not for the actual setting up – you can organise that yourself – but for the financial end of the day-to-day business.

As an incentive to draw in business, many accountants' first consultation is free. It will do you more good than harm to avail of such largesse. As you continue in business, you'll discover, there are all too few 'freebies' around!

Theoretically income tax is simple. All you need do is work out your total costs and take them away from your profits to arrive at your income, and bingo, there's your taxable income. Then send in your tax return.

This might work if you're a window cleaner, writer or driver. However, even at this level, you run the risk of paying too much tax, or claiming tax allowances on items you shouldn't. Not every business expense is tax deductible to the same degree and some are not at all.

The Pluses of Using an Accountant

An accountant will:

- find ways of raising capital
- set up cashflow forecasts and profit and loss forecasts
- advise whether you should register for VAT if you don't have to
- choose a starting date and, more importantly, a trading year end date
- keep day-to-day records, account books and ledgers
- claim all possible allowances and reliefs against tax and negotiate with the tax inspector
- claim expenses

- generally cope with financial matters

Finding the Right Accountant

There are accountants and then there are accountants. Many of them are fine book-keepers who will take your cardboard box full of assorted receipts, invoices, cheque stubs and statements and put them into order, calculate where you stand financially, work out your tax allowances and complete and send in your tax returns.

Others will offer a more thorough and expensive hands-on service, offering regular and invaluable advice and assistance.

If you don't already know a proven accountant – the best way to find one is by recommendation – call on a few local ones, tell them what you're about, ask if they will 'take you on' and what would be their charge? You will be able by discussion to decide the amount of work you want the accountant to do, the cost and the amount you'll do yourself.

It might work out cheaper just to hand over your paperwork every month while you get on with something else, but if you're determined to do it yourself and you have the time, energy and inclination at least at any given time you'll know exactly how your business stands.

The arrangement that appears to be best for people working from home is to do the books themselves, and then get the accountant to go over them every three or six months. This was the preferred method of the majority of people spoken to when researching this book. Your accountant will deal with your personal tax returns and integrate the figures to claim for everything you're entitled to.

Be warned. If you get involved in cash fiddles or dodgy deals, don't rely on your accountant to turn a blind eye. Certainly don't expect him to prepare and submit false accounts. You can really start worrying if he does! (See also Chapter 15 on tax and VAT.)

While employing an accountant does make life considerably easier, it is not absolutely necessary. However, if you decide not to use an accountant, you're going to have to be incredibly disciplined about keeping your finger on the pulse of every aspect of financial matters.

Next we'll explore the option of forming a limited company.

10

Forming a Limited Company

Many myths surround the phrase 'limited company' and many people, even those trading successfully, firmly believe that a limited company is not for them. But please read on and keep an open mind. When starting up any business – and earning your living from home is no different – it could be well worth your while looking into the feasibility of forming a limited company. The good news is that it can cost as little as £300.

The vast majority of companies set up in Ireland are known as 'two' companies, i.e. they have two shareholders, each holding one share. So the issue capital is two, with each shareholder holding 50 per cent equity of the company which means their liability is just that single share. At the same time the facility exists for the two shareholders to issue as many more shares as they wish out of their authorised share capital, which is usually about £1m, yes £1m.

Another option is the single-member company, first introduced to Ireland in October 1994. This is a private company incorporated with one subscriber and is seen as having the potential to give the entrepreneur greater flexibility regarding the manner in which the business is operated while still retaining appropriate safeguards for the wider business community.

If you're thinking of going the limited company route, it's recommended that you use an accountant in your business. Your accountant can handle the formalities of company formation or you can approach one of the several specialist formation agencies. You'll find them listed in the *Golden Pages*. Shop around and realise that not all packages are the same.

Formation Options

The company formation options listed below are courtesy of Inter Company Comparisons Limited (ICC):

- **Shelf Companies**

Ready-made (shelf) companies are held 'on the shelf' for instant use. Usually available are general trading, manufacturing, licensed premises, hotels, fashions, building, property, engineering, computers, investment and holding.

- **Special Formation**

Companies formed to your specification usually within a fortnight. This is achieved through the company using their Companies Office approved Memorandum and Articles of Association together with such variations as you may require, such as name, main objects clause, share capital, subscribers etc.

- **Guarantee Companies**

Companies where the members undertake on a winding up
to contribute (up to the limit of their guarantee) to the assets
of the company. These companies are usually charitable
bodies, flat management companies and sports clubs.

- **Unlimited Companies**

Do not give the benefit of limited liability to their members.
They are rarely used as trading entities, but may be used in
tax planning.

Advantages

For any business, including the small home operated one,
the main advantages to trading through a limited company
are the following:

- **Incorporation means limited liability**

It provides protection and is the cheapest form of insurance.
As discussed in previous chapters the majority of businesses
require borrowing, and we've all heard the harrowing stories
of homes being repossessed and worse, but if you trade
under a limited company you're liable only for your own
shareholding.

- **A company is a legal entity separate and distinct from its members**

Incorporation means that those involved are clothed with a corporate personality. The corporate person is quite separate and distinct from individual members of the enterprise. The company can sue and be sued in its own right.

- **Corporate identity security and credibility**

Another advantage of incorporation is that lending agencies are impressed by corporate identity. Within the current economic and financial climate in Ireland, for loan/grant purposes, rightly or wrongly, a limited company is regarded as having more security and credibility than the majority of private individuals.

- **Company's business is managed by directors**

This may not be applicable to the one man operation, but if your company gets larger, if desired, it frees members/shareholders from day-to-day involvement.

- **Incorporation affords a measure of name protection**

No two companies can be incorported with the same or similar name. The registration of business names provides no such measure of exclusivity.

One of the misconceptions about limited companies is that

you have to file detailed accounts annually. You have to file a return anyway and when you're a limited company what's required is a snapshot balance sheet, i.e. a basic statement of assets and liabilities. Profit and loss accounts are not necessary. Your accountant would prepare a special audit report which would be a general statement of the position of the company at that time.

It's about time we looked at the politics of working from home.

11

Home Politics

'Finality is not the language of politics,' said nineteenth-century British politician, Benjamin Disraeli, little thinking that a century later his words would equally apply to office and home politics.

We've all heard of office politics and know that to get on in our career, it's necessary to play them – and skilfully. What many people who're working from home don't realise, is that here too the game of politics has to be played with equal expertise.

As with office politics, home politics depend on listening to others' points of view, courtesy, consideration and realistic expectations. It isn't for nothing that the three Cs – Communication, Compromise and Commitment – are so often quoted.

The Three Cs

To implement the points listed below for successfully working from home, you're going to have to really *communicate* with the family; a certain amount of *compromise* on all sides is to be expected; and as for *commitment* – you'll have to prove your commitment to both your work, and to your family by:

- sticking to your schedule (whatever it is)
- keeping office hours (where possible)
- employing outside help (for gardening, housework)
- delegating (roping in the reluctant family)
- banning children from your office (the mutiny will pass)
- switching off (almost impossible)
- relaxing (teeth-clenchingly vital)
- keeping up contact with friends (worth the Houdini effort)
- escaping from the house (don't you want to remain sane?)

It's unlikely initially that you'll achieve all the points, but try for a few and, if you're lucky, the remainder might follow!

When you're in a relationship, be it marriage or living together, if both of you are used to working outside the home, there's less of a domestic upheaval when one of you decides to handle your career from home. But it's still essential to define boundaries from the beginning. Now that he's at home do you expect him to prepare dinner in the evenings? As she's there all day should she iron your shirts?

If your spouse/partner is used to being at home solo and you're going to base yourself there, no matter how great your relationship, there will be changes, probably some good, some bad. In Chapter 5, we looked at the more practical side of working from home. Here we're dealing with personalities and emotions.

It is easier when the decision to come in from outside is

made out of choice rather than necessity, as was the case with tapestry artist Angela Forte when she decided to concentrate on the creative side of her work; the same applies to Tony of Tony and Geraldine O'Daly (architects).

Others profiled, such as Brian Purcell (ostriches), Regina McGarrigle (teleworking), Tony O'Connell (electronic shopping mall), and the Mahers of Boyton Catering chose to operate from home. It makes sense for Joan Hanna (teddy bears) and Jill Aston (cakes) to be based at home and Cloona Health Centre owners, Dhara Kelly and Emer Gaffney, don't really have a choice.

But often the decision to work from home arises out of redundancy. Redundancy is trauma enough without the added implications of setting up, perhaps, a new business. You're used to the workplace culture – credibility, colleagues, working lunches, meetings, phones, faxes, modern technology, personal office space, a drink with your colleagues on the way home. When operating from home, you're reduced to isolation, insecurity, having to pay for every phone call. Think on. The list is endless.

Traditionally men have been more career-orientated than women and more used to being identified by what they do – Jack the doctor, Joe the builder. Only recently is this happening for women, but too often still they are primarily labelled wife and mother – Jack's wife, Joe junior's mother, rather than Jacqueline the gynaecologist, Josephine the interior designer!

The change from housewife to home-based careerist can require as much subtle politicising as going outside the home to work. The fabric of the household is going to change. It's foolish thinking otherwise. The family can no longer rely on having that apple tart on Fridays! Even the most caring modern man knows the quality of his life is better when his partner administers the household!

Children

The majority of children feel threatened by changing circumstances – during research we came across nine-year-old Emma who cried bitter tears when the hall door was painted red instead of its customary brown. Many children have an inbuilt ability to resist change with mulish passivity that results in negative chaos. When Rachel T. decided to set up office from home, her husband was all in favour, her children weren't. They wanted to know:

'If you're going to be working what about my rugby/hockey practice?'

'Who'll drive me to tennis/ballet?'

'I have to go to speech.'

'What about guides/scouts?'

(Up to now they'd been vehemently opposed to any of these extramural activities.)

Next came the blackmailing power of food. 'What about my sandwiches? Will you still make them?' Rachel had made them every day for years and knew they were invariably disposed of uneaten in a variety of ways. 'What about my dinner? Who'll get it for me?' The daily battles since they'd left the breast were legion. At this stage their memories of home cuisine were golden and they envisaged a famine-like future. But they survived and five years on are vocally grateful when she makes an apple tart!

Up and Running

From the beginning you have to be businesslike. No matter who turns up on the doorstep during your working hours wondering if you'd like to take a run in the car he's thinking of buying, have a game of golf or break for a coffee, you're going to have to say something like, 'Thanks, but no. I'm working, but I'd be delighted to . . .', and make a date. They'll soon get the message and if they don't you can't afford to have them in your working life.

You've got over the first hurdle of getting going. But working out of the family home, while it has many benefits, also has hidden snags. If you're counselling in your front room, you can't have toddlers playing Darth Vader in the hall or teenagers blaring music in the family room.

Suppose you plan to operate an accountancy service from the spare bedroom. It'll be difficult to think, much less concentrate on figures, if you're surrounded by the thumping high jinks of showering and hairwashing. Even if your surgery is separate from the house, as the majority of doctors' and dentists' are, it's extremely unprofessional to have the usual family noises filtering in from the garden.

Hogging the phone is one of the biggest bones of contention, particularly with teenagers. It's not possible to operate a business without phone access.

After years of trying to make do with one line for family and business, a freelance photographer says getting his own line was the best decision he ever made and it was surprisingly inexpensive. Installation of the extra line cost in the region of £100 and was carried out within 10 days of putting in the request.

When you've operated as a close family where sharing is taken for granted, difficulties can arise when Jimmy, playing games on your computer, loses data or Mary, who starts by studying in your office, gradually moves in complete with music, cans, crisps and friends. When you deny her further access, she'll make you feel as guilty as hell. Stick to your guns about your office being out of bounds. Close your ears to her arguments. It's a battle you have to win.

If you're the one who has kept the house ticking over, you'll have to learn to close the door of your workplace on unmade beds, a car that needs washing, a sink full of dishes and grass to be mowed.

If your budget is tight – and it usually is when you're starting up – but if it can be stretched to just one luxury, how about employing somebody to do the house even once a week? Even if you're only minimally house-proud, there's no greater joy than to emerge from a day's work to be met by the wafting scent of Mr Sheen, dishless sinks, plumped cushions and carpets minus dog hairs.

Another pitfall to watch out for is neglect of the family. If the conversation isn't scintillating and there's work to be done, it is all too easy to wander into your office and close the door. The ideal working from home situation is where you keep office hours five days a week. It's almost impossible to achieve.

Jean's Memories

'My abiding memory of childhood is going to sleep to the sound of Dad's typewriter. I loved it, it was hypnotic, relaxing and I always felt safe with him nearby,' says Jean. When she was twelve, the success of her father's third book enabled him to leave his teaching job to work full-time from home on fiction.

'By osmosis we became familiar with the business of writing books – we knew the highs and lows, we discussed royalties, agents, foreign markets, publishers, take overs. We loved the intrigues.

'Just as well because I think no matter what you work at from the home there's no such thing as a total switch off.

'In theory it's ideal to separate work from family. In practice it's almost impossible, particularly with something as internally consuming as writing.

'Dad tried to be punctilious about writing for a mimimum of six hours, five days a week. But he often broke his working code to come to our hockey matches and amateur theatricals. Indeed he was more visible than the majority of fathers, but we'd give him a hard time if he didn't turn up. Because he was there, we didn't take his work seriously.

'Now that I'm in an office environment, one thing I'm sure of and have been for years is that I'll always go out to work. I'm even reluctant to bring papers home.

'Despite the benefits of having Dad working from home – like always being on hand to mend a puncture or to drive us places and good humouredly, it caused problems.

'As well as living with his success, we had to live with

his worries when plots weren't working out and book sales weren't as high as anticipated.

'When you're working with others you have to be diplomatic. You can't snap at them if they forget to give you a message, or threaten to kill them if they borrow your stapler – the rationale being that you have to continue working with these people. Dad reserved no such diplomacy for us.

'We all acquired business skills and learned how to deal with people. We had to. He expected us to perform better in the taking of messages/dealing with contacts/respect for his workplace than any secretary.

'I never remember him being really relaxed or switched off about his work. And we found it difficult to keep the barrier between work and family that he required. His office was out of bounds and his equipment was *verboten* and we hated it.

'With hindsight as an adult I can see the many difficulties he had with the blurring together of writing and family; the interruptions that must have broken his train of thought. His commitment to each project was total. It was only years later that I realised the long hours he put in and how hard he worked. I'm certain my own work ethic was acquired from him.'

Now that we've seen that the working from home syndrome isn't all necessarily rosy, in Chapter 12 we're going to look at what happens when plans don't work out and you have to rethink and re-strategise your career.

12

When You Have to Rethink

Sometimes even the best laid plans just don't work out. When this happens the wise entrepreneur cuts losses and gets out, subscribing to the theory that there is no point in flogging a dead horse. This is one of the abilities that separates the winners from the losers, the survivors from the defeated, the strong from the weak. Take another look at 'Risk Taking' and 'Dealing with Failure' in Chapter 2.

There are some ideas that have an enduring appeal for the budding entrepreneur. To the uninitiated, they seem to require no special training, and they bring you into contact with areas generally associated with pleasure.

These include having a bookshop, a professorial type of dream; catering pub grub, a constant atmosphere of conviviality; being a newsagent, a back-to-basics, part of the community type operation; owning a boutique, the realisation of many a woman's fantasy but rightly dubbed 'the housewife's folly'; and running an employment agency, how gratifying to be instrumental in assisting people realise their career dreams.

But some of the people interviewed who followed such

paths without the right training and with insufficient market research, initially have had their fingers burned. In true entrepreneurial style they had the ability to recognise and to rise above their mistake and to rethink and redirect themselves.

Bookseller

Roger R.'s dream was to own a bookshop. He loved books, handling them, reading them; he even loved the people he met who were similarly interested. He and his wife Eileen were both teachers and when they retired, with the family reared, educated and gone, they determined to realise Roger's dream. The plan was to start off by selling second-hand all those interesting books Roger had acquired over the years. The reality wasn't so.

They scoured a radius of twenty miles in the midlands where they lived for a suitable premises of a shop on the ground floor and living accommodation above. When they found it after six months, they sold the family home, used the extra money to make the necessary conversions and set up in business with great optimism and enthusiasm.

Roger soon learned that his love of books wasn't enough. Running a bookshop has its perils and pitfalls as well as its rewards. An understanding of retailing in general is essential, as well as a good knowledge of the way the book trade works. Roger had neither. These skills are necessary to make a success of running an independent bookshop at a time when the chain and multiple bookshops are growing in number and in strength.

Net profit in bookselling is notoriously low. Publishers offer the retailer set discount rates, which can vary from publisher to publisher and from book to book (in Ireland the rate is usually between 35 per cent and 45 per cent). Larger orders carry larger discounts, but it is a gamble to buy in a large number of copies on the chance of a potential bestseller, though to be fair most books are sold on a sale or return basis. As Roger soon discovered no bookseller can stock more than a fraction of the hundreds of thousands of titles in print.

At this time the Net Book Agreement was still observed in Ireland. This meant that booksellers in general abided by publishers' prices, so price competition was not a feature of the book trade. Instead, the emphasis had to be on stock and service. An independent bookseller like Roger had to learn what to stock for the needs of the community, particularly in a rural area. Since the demise of the NBA, the greatest threat to small booksellers is the discounting power of multiples and bigger shops.

After a hairy year's trading, Roger and Eileen took stock of their business and made a firm decision to deal in books in areas they both knew. After visiting the local schools and discussing booklists with the principals, they decided to focus primarily on school books, children and teen fiction and non-fiction and a limited selection of popular fiction and non-fiction, chosen to appeal to the parents. Once they had carried out and implemented their market research, the business took a turn for the better.

Pub Grub

When Jane and Dessie B. married, Dessie's father suggested they live above the pub that Dessie had been managing for several years. It seemed an ideal solution. The upper two storeys were revamped and modernised to provide suitable living accommodation, including a second kitchen, as Jane planned to develop the catering end of the business.

She had worked in the local bank for six years but always dreamed of operating her own business. She wanted to build up the pub food end, which had existed for the past three years as little more than packaged cheese sandwiches, cellophaned slabs of fruit cake, packets of biscuits and the ubiquitous crisps.

The idea was good in theory but it needed to be followed through with market analysis and training. Jane's main mistake was expecting to be able to start her business without any knowledge of the intricacies of catering – the buying, the cooking, gauging quantities, staffing, presentation and serving.

It also would have helped if she had an overview of the pub trade. She learned the hard way and luckily it was her pride more than the business that was dinted. But the one area she shone in from the beginning was balancing the books!

Newsagent

Running a small shop that sells newspapers and magazines as well as sweets and cigarettes is not an easy life, nor an outstandingly lucrative one as Sandra K., a single parent with two children aged four and six, discovered. Before she took over the newsagency in the suburbs of Dublin, she checked the lease and the standing of the business and ensured that the wholesaler who supplied the previous owner would continue to supply her. She found out, among other things, that there was nothing automatic about this.

There were limitations on the numbers of papers she could buy on sale or return, and some magazines were supplied on firm sale only – easy to find yourself with unsold stock.

Sandra had to open every day newspapers appeared, otherwise she would lose sales. She had to be up before the lark each morning – difficult with two small children who never slept the night through – taking delivery of the papers, sorting them and marking them when she started a delivery round. Among her headaches was sending out bills to tardy payers, explaining to customers why their newspaper or magazine hadn't arrived – which could be due to bad weather, or industrial action.

She thought home delivery would make things easier, but it proved a nightmare. It was difficult to find reliable schoolchildren to do her rounds, and she often ended up packing her own two in their pyjamas into the car and making the rounds herself before returning to get them dressed, breakfasted and to school. Then she would officially open the shop.

Sweets and tobacco, being tempting, pocketable and anonymous, are readily stolen. Selling requires sharp-eyed vigilance both in the stockroom and in the shop. Sandra had to deal with numerous suppliers offering such a diversity of lines that she discovered there was a need for constant stock checks and reordering. Access to a computer became necessary as the prices she was allowed to charge changed with surprising frequency. It wasn't unusual for her to work a ninety-hour week and she no better than made a living.

When she was offered a well-paying job managing a newsgency in a large shopping centre, she took it gratefully, putting her entrepreneurial instincts on hold until her children are older.

Boutique Owner

From the time Anne G. was seventeen she worked in ladies fashion in one of London's best known department stores. She was a good sales lady, graduated to buyer and had an instinctive knowledge of what suited her clients, with the result that they returned season after season. It was when they began bringing their daughters that she decided to take the option of early retirement, return to the west of Ireland and open her own fashion boutique.

She delegated to her brother the task of finding a suitable premises including living accommodation and approved unequivocally of his choice. After sussing out the local competition and discovering it was almost non-existent, she was even more confident. Within two years she reckoned she'd have cornered the market. She had a healthy nestegg saved and had no trouble getting additional funding from the local bank where her family had been customers for generations.

She had her own ideas about decor and employed a local builder who interpreted them to her satisfaction. After a buying trip to Europe and heavy local media coverage, she had a champagne opening, which spilled out into the street and went on until midnight. From beginning to end it had all gone like a dream.

Next day when she opened for business her dream ended and reality began. The locals stayed away in their droves. It wasn't that they didn't like her clothes. It was just that they continued frequenting the shops where they'd always gone. They were friendly when she met them in the street, coming out of Mass, visiting the family home.

After two years, she decided to cut her losses and to retire from commercial life. To her delight the premises sold at a substantial profit, she bought a small bungalow and has taken to growing roses with great enthusiasm.

Employment Agency

When Jimmy L., personnel manager in a private company, was made redundant, one night after consuming several pints, he decided to open an employment agency. Analysis in the cold light of next morning did nothing to change his mind. Little did he realise that even with his skills and experience, it was a far from easy project.

He was trained in the business, had the requisite skills such as sales ability, interviewing techniques, contacts, computer literacy, an abundance of patience and, most importantly, he was able to relate to all sorts of people. Also, he was familiar with the various statutes and regulations concerning employers and employees. He planned to focus on an office agency, including secretarial, clerical and temporary in the same categories.

He got his licence from the Department of Enterprise and Employment without hassle. The licence fee is £400 per annum and one of the main criteria is to have enough space to interview privately prospective candidates for jobs. He rented premises with a shopfront in the south suburbs of Dublin and moved in on the first floor himself, all the better being on the spot to run the business.

His first mistake was not carrying out any form of market research, his second was relying mainly on past contacts, his third was hard selling his applicants to his clients and vice versa. He ended up alienating both parties by sending unsuitable applicants to clients in the hope of doing business.

While he did display the job vacancies in the window, when he wasn't getting immediate results, he ran up unnecessary advertising bills in the newspapers. He skimped on keeping records up to date. Too late he discovered that running an employment agency on his own without the back-up of a large corporation such as he was used to involved a great deal of record-keeping – more than enough record keeping, paperwork and book-keeping to keep one person fully occupied.

He decided not to prolong the agony and closed the business within nine months. When last heard of, Jimmy and a school friend were successfully operating a chauffeur service.

Money matters next. In Chapter 13 we deal with keeping track of money and, even more importantly, getting in money.

13

Money Matters

'Money is like a sixth sense without which you cannot make a complete use of the other five,' believed W. Somerset Maugham, better known for his writing than for his business acumen. But he certainly had the right idea – you can't survive personally without keeping money matters in order. You certainly can't run any sort of a business without punctilious attention to all matters appertaining to money.

Keeping Track

No matter what our role in life it's necessary to budget, to keep track of our spending, to spend within income, and to make sure we get in our money. In business it's vital. Lack of financial control, more than any other factor, is the downfall of business. Keeping track of the inflows and outflows of money is not complicated – it's mainly common sense. It's usually done by filing documents relating to transactions and recording information in various books of account. The type of system used to a large extent depends on the type of business.

A book-keeping system need not be elaborate or sophisticated to do the job. The double entry system, devised centuries ago, gives precise control of your business whether in a ledger or on a computer and allows immediate access to your financial status. Each transaction is entered twice so when you, say, buy a calculator, you record separately the purchase and the amount it cost.

Computer software accountancy packages, such as Take-5, meet most of the requirements of a small business. The ideal system should be simple enough to allow you to keep records up to date with minimum effort and be capable of providing the right information to enable you to run and control your business.

How about this for a sinister verse?

His VAT is all messy
His books they won't tot
His biro is empty
It's past twelve o'clock
His accountant is angry
The taxman will call
The sheriff is lurking
Is there no cure at all?

Depending on your cash situation, your method can be as simple as what's often called current account trading, though it has to be said that such financial simplicity is not suitable for many businesses. For current account trading:

- use a credit card or cheque book for expenditure
- arrange with your bank to pay regular bills by standing order or direct debit
- withdraw your cash requirements either weekly or monthly (keep an itemised statement of expenditure)
- lodge monies received (keeping a detailed lodgement slip)

If opting for current account trading, use a duplicate cheque book where you have a carbon copy of each cheque written. Completed cheque stubs act as a record of your payments. If it's not automatic with your bank, it's a good idea to get a printout of your account position at least once every two months. Some banks have reduced their frequency of sending out statements.

The advantage of credit cards is that at a cost of £30.00 per annum, you can get up to six weeks' interest free after purchase and also a limited overdraft facility linked into your credit limit. The downside of credit cards is that if bills aren't paid in full each month, interest is charged in the region of 22.5 per cent per annum, or 24.92 per cent APR (Annual Percentage Rate). Detailed credit card statements are issued monthly.

Getting In Money

It's all fine having perfect records, being up to date in your money administration, but the most important aspect of any business is actually getting in overdue monies. Nearly everyone in business on their own will have come across the reluctant payers. It's a delicate and decidedly 'Catch 22' situation. You've to acquire the money without alienating your client. How to go about it without causing offence can be the problem.

Betty K.'s Story

Betty's area of expertise is compiling brochures for companies, hotels, trade shows. A certain hotel invited her to complete a brochure in time for the opening of their new facilities. Betty's *modus operandi* is to subcontract the photography and design and to do the writing of the brochure herself.

Her initial meeting with her clients gives her an idea of their expectations and the amount of money they're prepared to spend. 'I've come across people who think they can have a full colour brochure for a total spend of £500,' she says. 'I sort out accommodation for "away" deals at the first meeting. For instance, with a hotel brochure like this, I clarify whether the photographer and I can overnight in the hotel, with breakfast, snacks (within reason) and dinner as part of the deal. I make sure that my clients understand that good photography requires the right weather conditions, which could result in an extra day's shoot.'

After years of experience in such negotiations, Betty favours a day rate, including an agreed number of meetings and two proofings, which she confirms in writing. 'If you settle on a flat rate for the finished job, some clients think you can spend your time attending meetings and at the drop of a hat, change job specification on their flimsiest whim and generally be at their beck and call until the job is finished.'

Betty requests 30 per cent of her fee up front, but seldom receives it; specifies payment within 30 days of invoice and usually gets it, out of which she pays for the photography, design and printing.

When the agreement is finalised, she confirms in writing. She then contacts the photographer, discussing photographic requirements, such as numbers, sizes and colour, also fee and expenses. When doing a hotel brochure, she needs to know whether the photographer requires an advance recce to work out shots and special requirements such as flower arrangements, tables laid, certain food prepared – some foods photograph better than others. A day rate fee is agreed.

She has worked with the same designer, who prints in-house, for years, and they understand each other. She usually alerts him that there's a job on the agenda, with deadline date and outline requirements. They agree a fee. If the deal is cancelled a cancellation fee – percentage of total agreed in advance, plus expenses incurred to date – becomes payable by the client.

Betty and the photographer work in tandem – in some cases the text dictating the photographs, sometimes *vice versa.* She writes the script and takes it and the photographs to the designer who puts together a mock-up, which she then brings in person to the clients for proofing. They also approve final copy before printing.

The compilation of the brochure for this particular hotel went like a dream. The clients were amiable and easy to deal with, the opening was a grand success and the brochure received extravagant compliments.

But four months later, Betty still hadn't received payment. Monthly statements and weekly telephone calls were ignored and she was reluctant to send a solicitor's letter, as she rightly felt it could be the kiss of death to other business in the locality.

Finally, taking the bull by the horns, she drove to the hotel and arrived unannounced one holiday weekend. They expressed themselves delighted to see her, but she detected an uneasiness in them. She told them she had been passing and would pick up her fee. They said it wasn't convenient right then.

She answered she'd wait until it was, that she'd have tea in the lounge, perhaps a swim, even stay the night if they still hadn't dealt with the matter of her cheque. She wasn't happy with her method of collection but getting in her fee was her priority. She received it before she had drunk her second cup of tea and lodged it first thing on Tuesday morning.

Payment

It's an ideal, but not usual, situation to get cash with order. On certain Irish publications, the journalists got together and insisted; they now receive a third of the fee on commission and complete payment on receipt of copy.

In theory you can insist on a pro forma invoice, but it's likely that by doing so, in today's competitive climate, you'll lose a lot of business. A pro forma invoice is where you, as vendor, require payment before delivery of goods. To achieve this the invoice is issued to the customer giving details of payment necessary to obtain goods/service. This will include the selling price plus, where applicable, trade discount and additional charges for postage and packing.

The next method, and one that's frequently used, is to offer your customers a generous discount for quick payment This may be anything from 10 per cent for payment within seven days to 2.5 per cent if it's in one month. Before you do this, make sure you can afford such a generous gesture.

Then there's the personal phone call to the principal involved. This can be an effective way of either severing your relationship or getting your money, depending on the client, his personality and type of day he's having.

Last, but very effective, as Betty K. and many others have discovered, is the personal call. To do this successfully you have to have the gumption and the determination to carry it through. Never give the impression, whether it's true or not, that the money is necessary to put the next litre of petrol in your car. Dress the part of success – don't make the mistake Anne R. did on her first visit to her bank manager for the loan to start up her crèche. Be prepared to sit on and on and on. This method is particularly effective in a case like Betty's where she was in a public place and could have, if she so wished, struck up a 'friendly' conversation with the residents!

Next we'll look at selling.

14

Selling

So you've had enough positive feedback from your testing of the market (Chapter 6) to go ahead, but remember your product or service cannot be put on the market in isolation. You've to consider to whom, how, when and where you're going to sell. Selling is the ultimate function of marketing.

To a large extent, the nature of the product or service dictates the finding of your customers. Child minding requires children, woollen sweaters are for people, filing systems for offices, window frames for the building industry or DIY-er.

Ideally you should consider distribution and selling before you start into manufacturing. If you've ready-made buyers, clients and customers, nurture and guard them like gold dust.

Via Shops

- Make an appointment to see the owner/manager; don't just turn up unannounced.
- Familiarise yourself with competing products and prices,

so that you can point out the advantages of yours.

- Be clear about your price but willing to allow the retailer an attractive discount. The main problem is to decide whether to sell on sale or return or not.
- Prove you can guarantee supplies and stick to delivery dates.
- Package your product attractively; think about display aids.

Direct Approach

- Your best weapon is a detailed knowledge of your product and the ability to explain and if necessary demonstrate.
- Keep detailed accounts of your customers as well as how much they buy, not overlooking their preferences.
- Be in constant touch, but not so often that they feel hounded, so that when your customers think of buying they automatically think of you.
- Get feedback.
- Treat complaints in a friendly spirit; put anything right that needs rectifying.

Mail Order

A system by which customers order and the goods are sent direct to them – Simone Stephenson is using this method as another selling prong for her bird houses. Payment is usually by cheque or credit card with order and it's usual to offer free approval – money back if not satisfied.

Products suitable for mail order selling should be:

- light in weight, but strong enough not to break in transit
- not obtainable in ordinary retail shops
- more expensive in shop

Through an Agent

Advantages

- additional sales
- being informed on competition

Disadvantages

- agent's commission reduces your profit

If you're selling as a retailer, middleman, agent or dealer you've little influence on the actual form of the product. But if it's something you've designed and produced, such as cakes (Jill Aston), portraits (Anne O'Shea), candles (Ciaran Ganter), teddy bears (Joan Hanna), tapestries (Angela Forte), it's up to you to decide the final form. Don't fall in love with the original idea and insist on going through with it, impervious to the demands of the market.

Mary R.'s Story

Like Mary R., be flexible. She started painting silk as an occupational therapy while recovering from an operation. She did no market research, had no product expertise, knew nothing about selling, yet within six months demand was outpacing supply.

She began by making one size only hand-painted silk scarves; then a friend asked her to make a specific size, another for a cravat, someone else for a decorative pocket handkerchief. Without even knowing it, she was rising to the occasion by meeting market demand for painting on silk, but hadn't a clue how to go about it.

She enrolled in a one-day workshop, by five o'clock had painted her first scarf, was bitten by the bug and as happens in the best of stories never looked back. Recently she has bought a steamer, so that she can set the colours herself and she employs a local woman to handroll the edges. (Mary's scarves are no more than a commercial hobby.)

Your product can be produced in several versions with varying functions at different price levels; it can be highly specialised with only one use, or several functions can be incorporated to widen its appeal; it can be made part of a range of related products; the material from which it is made can be changed; or it can be scrapped and started over again.

Remember it may be unwise to include every possible refinement right from the start – a highly specialised product may appeal only to a small market. A simpler version may sell better and pave the way for a more complex one. A typical example are the mugs of potter, Dave Dain, which he regards as both the yardstick and foundation of his business and the means of more creative experimentation.

If your product requires the skills of different people, as

often happens, say, in the case of restoring antiques, you need to make sure from the start that you can depend on your labour. Both Simone Stephenson (bird houses) and Patrick Quilligan (mobile computer desks) put in a lot of legwork locating craft people specifically to fulfil their requirements.

Arthur N.'s Story

A hiccup, particularly when the self-employed employ, can be positively damaging to your reputation, as Arthur N. discovered.

When Arthur retired he turned his lifelong interest and hobby in antiques to a home-based business. He began tracking down and buying commissioned pieces, which eventually led to him bidding for items requiring restoration.

At a house auction, Arthur secured for a lady client a nineteenth-century English chest. She was delighted when he suggested having minor repairs carried out prior to handing it over to her, but the work, undertaken for Arthur by a craftsman, was not up to standard. A costly item of furniture was reduced in value, but even worse for Arthur he had a dissatisfied customer.

Another point to consider – Is your product seasonal?

The most wonderfully exotic, delicious plum puddings are likely to sell only around Christmas, so if you're going into the cookery business, ideally you'll need several bread and butter – excuse the pun! – lines to keep ticking over.

Selling Services

As author, lecturer, businessman Christopher Temple points out in his book *Working From Home,* when you're selling a service plus your own expertise it's as important to define it as precisely as a product.

Suppose you're basing a security business from home you've to decide whether you'll supply a delivery service complete with armoured cars, human guards, guard dogs; or offer specialist advice on how people can improve the security of their house or factory.

In the case of consultancy or agency work it's also necessary to define your scope as clearly as possible. When setting up as a consultant, you're more likely to succeed if you limit your field to where your particular expertise lies. Rather than grandly planning to become an import-export agent, aim, in the beginning anyway, to trade with specific products in a specific area.

Another important factor to bear in mind with regard to service orientated businesses is that many of them do not require a large amount of capital, therefore the business can start from such humble beginnings as one or two jobs and grow from there. This applies to building on a small scale, gardening, decorating, keyboard skills, child minding – services that are often based locally, with satisfied customers providing unlimited free publicity.

After all this selling, we can no longer avoid taking a look at tax and VAT.

15

Tax and VAT

Income Tax

Albert Einstein isn't the only person to express the sentiment that, 'The hardest thing in the world to undersand is income tax.' Since income tax came into being during the nineteenth century, it has been a bone of contention and a cause of worry for endless business people.

The main problem is that over the years we've listened to the bad press that tax receives, and built up a resistance without even taking the time to study it. We dismiss it as difficult, impossible and complicated. Once you acquire even a basic understanding, you'll realise it's none of these things. If you're going to set up on your own you'll need to learn the rudiments of income tax, which requires only an input of your time and patience.

In business it's vital from the word go to handle your income tax professionally. Contrary to public perception, income tax officials exist to help rather than just to catch out the general public.

Before you go too far in the initial organisation of your business it's advisable to visit your nearest tax office (listed in the front of telephone directories under Revenue Commissioners). There you can acquire relevant information, have a preliminary discussion with one of the officials, and be advised as to your requirements. If you've paid tax previously under PAYE or by direct payment, you'll retain the same number, so make sure to have it with you; and it's a good idea to have your queries listed in writing.

If it's a quiet office and off-peak tax time, you'll likely be dealt with immediately, but in a busy office, you'll be given a number and will have to wait until it is called.

The self-assessment system, introduced in 1988/89, gives the self-employed and people receiving rental or investment incomes control and responsibility for their income tax. It presumes you deal with your tax affairs honestly. You have a legal duty to make a tax return every year.

It's up to you to:

- Advise your tax office when you become chargeable to tax, e.g. when you begin a business. You'll be given a Revenue and Social Insurance Number (RSI Number).
- Keep accurate records of all business/financial trans-actions so that a true profit income figure can be calculated for tax purposes.
- Operate PAYE/PRSI on payments made to employees (unlikely to apply when you're starting up business from home, but do keep it in mind for when you expand).
- Register for VAT if your level of business/services requires it (see below).

Keeping Records

You will have to keep sufficient records to make a true return of your income. Simply keeping bank statements is not enough. The 'double entry' book keeping system covered in Chapter 13 gives you complete control of your business. All records must be kept for six years. The type of records you keep depends on your business and yourself – take advice from your accountant, if you're using one – but must include:

- goods and services (where relevant) bought and sold
- money received and paid out
- supporting records, such as invoices, bank statements, cheque stubs

Your records must show the amount and source of:

- all income
- all purchases and other outgoings

Preliminary Tax

Under the self-assessment system you're obliged to:

- Pay preliminary tax on or before 1 November each year.
- Make your tax return after the end of your tax year, but not later than 31 January following the end of the tax year.
- Pay any balance of tax due on receipt of assessment.

Preliminary tax is your estimate of the income tax payable by you for the year, remembering that it includes PRSI, health contribution and, if applicable, income levy and employment and training levy. Although you probably won't be able to estimate your final amount of tax, make sure that the preliminary payment is not less than the lower of:

• your final liability for the previous year

or

• 90 per cent of your liability for the current year

If you don't pay by 1 November, or if you under-pay, you're charged interest at the rate of 1.25 per cent per month or part of.

Making Tax Returns

It's your responsibility to make sure that you get, complete and return your tax return no later than 31 January after the year of assessment. From a business point of view the earlier you submit after the end of the tax year the sooner you will know the final amount you've to pay, important when you come to paying preliminary tax.

You'll be assessed in accordance with your return and this assessment will show your total tax liability for the year, i.e. income tax, PRSI, health contribution and levies. The preliminary tax which you've already paid will be credited.

Basis of Assessment

Your tax assessment is normally based on your income from 6 April to the following 5 April. For those of you in your first year of business, your assessment is based on profits from the date you started to the following 5 April. In your second year, assessment will be twelve months from start up date.

Farmers' Self-Assessment

In general the system for farmers is similar to that used for other types of business. But the special provision remains where farmers may assess their profits as the average profit over three years. If you're a farmer and you opt for averaging, the deadline before which averaging may be cancelled has been extended to the return filing date (i.e. 31 January in the year following the end of the relevant tax year).

Revenue Audit

A revenue audit is an examination by a revenue official of a taxpayer's tax returns and records to ensure that all profits and other income are correctly calculated and returned. An audit may also be carried out to check the validity of claimed allowances and reliefs. Each year a number of taxpapers are selected, some randomly, others because their return doesn't look right, others still because of a tip-off.

Value Added Tax (VAT)

VAT is a tax on sales and services supplied in the course of business. The current annual limits are:
* £32,000 if you're supplying goods
* £15,000 for services

If you're liable for tax and if your turnover exceeds the above, you must register for VAT. You may elect to register for VAT:

* if, as a trader, you can pass on a VAT credit
* if you're dealing in zero rated goods, such as food, you can claim VAT incurred on purchases and business expenses.

You can apply for VAT registration by filling out a VAT 1 form, available from any tax office, and returning it to any tax office.

VAT is incurred on goods and services acquired for the business and charged on goods and services supplied by the business. If you're registered, you're liable to pay the difference between VAT charged and VAT incurred. Equally, you'll be paid if the amount of VAT incurred exceeds the amount charged.

Adequate books and records must be kept so that your VAT position can be clearly established. As with income tax, unless you're told otherwise, records must be kept for six years. In addition to having properly written up and regularly balanced books of account, you must keep invoices, credit and debit notes, receipts, vouchers and other supporting

VAT documentation.

Every two months, you'll receive a VAT 3 form, unless you've agreed to account for VAT on an annual basis. You must complete and return this form, together with VAT, payable not later than the nineteenth of the month after the end of the two-month period in question. The form must give details of:

- VAT incurred for the period
- VAT charged for the period
- (if applicable) Goods supplied to/received from other member states of the EU

In addition, a single annual return giving trading details – annual sales and purchases – is required.

We'll finish Part I with pensions and insurance.

16

Pensions and Insurance

Far too many of us working from home don't even think of pensions, much less critical illness cover, and when our accountant, solicitor or family friends raise the question, as people with our best interests at heart will, we'll often prevaricate.

It's easy to justify prevarication by being too busy, so absorbed in our work that what spare time we have is precious and to be used for leisure and family. Even to think of retirement or being unable to work might change our luck. And so we can go from month to month, year to year with what is an irresponsible attitude and an inefficient handling of our affairs – rather like the people who think making a will could hasten their demise!

Often we'll tell ourselves it's better to think positively and get on with the job, but as you should have gathered by now, to earn your living successfully from home means being realistic. When we're working for ourselves, we owe it to ourselves and our families to take care of such matters.

The sooner we make provision for some form of pension the better, as the older we get the more expensive pensions become. As mentioned earlier, with increased redundancies and unemployment more and more people are working from home and often starting in their middle years which can be vulnerable enough without the added trauma of job change and financial insecurity.

While many will have pensions securely in place, others may have difficulties about continuing payments. Others again either won't have a pension or it won't be transferrable.

'Pensions and insurance are expensive and value for money is essential,' says Tony Moore, who set up his own consultancy business after being made redundant. 'No matter how desirable it is to have an adequate pension at sixty the money has to be available and often, particularly in the initial stages of start up, it can be a choice between paying the mortgage or the premium.'

It's the wise person who looks pragmatically at all eventualities. It's a fact that the majority of us are less active at sixty than we were at thirty, yet with improved lifestyle and advances in medical technology many of us will enjoy life into our eighties.

When we decide to take life easier, wind down the business, work reduced hours, hopefully we'll have more to look forward to than life on the limited income you get with a state pension, which currently for a single person is £69 per week and £112 for a married couple.

The best initial course of action is to list in writing what you hope to achieve from a pension. A formal pension does not necessarily have to be taken out. Have you thought about regular savings, accruing interest over the coming years that could shape into an income when you decide to retire? For instance Post Office saving certificates, currently on the twelfth issue are state guaranteed. Money deposited for five years and nine months is guaranteed a 40 per cent return, the equivalent of 6 per cent per annum.

Discuss the various options and your requirements with your bank or building society manager and talk to a few of the major insurance companies – you'll find a selection listed in the *Golden Pages* under Insurance. Representatives will be only too delighted to do business with you, but remember, they're primarily salespeople, earning their living by selling policies to you.

Listen to and analyse the advice from the experts. But before committing yourself make sure whatever option you choose, as far as possible, meets your requirements.

Pensions

Now that you've shopped around, it's time to look at the benefits of a personal retirement plan; as well as peace of mind, it's a tax-efficient way of looking to your future. There's tax relief on your contributions; tax-free growth on your investment; and, usually at between the ages of sixty and seventy, a 25 per cent tax-free lump sum, with the remaining 75 per cent being used to buy a pension to provide you with guaranteed income for the remainder of your life. The level of your pension depends on:

- the size of fund available to buy pension
- the type of pension you want
- annuity rates at the time

A pension can be bought in your own name or in the joint names of you and your spouse. If the pension is in joint names part of it can continue to be paid to your spouse after your death. The pension can be level or escalating and will be guaranteed for life; also it can have a guaranteed minimum payout period of up to ten years.

Pension or 'annuity' rates determine how much pension you will get at retirement for each £1,000 of accumulated funds. These rates tend to move in line with interest rates, although once you buy your pension the rate is fixed for life. Some pension plans contain an 'open market' option, which means that when you come to buy your pension you can shop around various life assurance companies to get the best value.

Usually extra benefits can be added to protect your dependants against the financial consequences of your premature death or serious ill health. If you die before you take your retirement plan, benefits the value of your plan at that stage will be paid to your estate.

Next is a sample personal pension plan, courtesy of Norwich Union:

Personal details – female, aged 40 next birthday, pension age 60, non-smoker, tax rate 48 per cent.

Pension Contribution, Indexation 5 per cent:

Initial gross monthly premium (21 years' payments)		£ 100.00
Less tax relief of		£ 48.00
Net monthly premium		£ 52.00

Guaranteed Retirement Benefits:

Guaranteed retirement fund £ 20,229 plus bonuses

Illustrative Retirement benefits	@ 9% p.a.	@ 10% p.a.
Estimated fund	£84,136	£93,503
Providing pension of	£ 8,161 p.a.	£ 9,070 p.a.
or		
Tax free cash of	£21,034 p.a	£23,376 p.a.
plus reduced pension of	£ 6,121 p.a.	£ 6,802 p.a.

On death before retirement, premiums paid are returned in full

Additional Level Term Insurance Cover:

Sum insured to age 60		£20,000.00
Gross monthly premium (20 years' payments)	£	10.00
Less tax relief of	£	4.80
Net monthly premium	£	5.20

Total monthly premium in first year, gross £110.00; net £57.20

The above illustrations are based on the assumed gross rates of return on premiums received as shown, at an assumed investment period of 20.5 years.

The illustrative pensions are payable monthly in arrears, guaranteed payable for five years and life thereafter and assume an annuity rate of 9.7 per cent is available at retirement. The actual amount payable may be greater or less than shown.

The illustrative retirement benefits assume premiums are indexed by 5 per cent. Assuming current premium rates are maintained this policy will provide a With Profit Retirement Fund of £34,265, excluding bonuses, at the pension age.

Tax relief on pension premiums is limited to 15 per cent of net relevant earnings. Net relevant earnings means earned income net of expenses such as mortgage interest. Tax relief on death benefit premiums is limited to 5 per cent of net relevant earnings and death benefit premiums are aggregated with pension premiums for the purpose of the overall 15 per cent limit on contributions.

A non-smoker is defined as a person who has not smoked any form of tobacco in the last year and does not intend doing so in the future.

Critical Illness Protection

Critical Illness Protection is relatively new to the Irish market. It's offered automatically by some companies when you're buying a pension. It's worth looking into. One of the worst things that can happen in life is that you become seriously ill. The implications are much worse when you're self-employed. The facts are:

- Over 13,000 people in Ireland are diagnosed as having cancer each year – five years after diagnosis of a life threatening cancer, 35 per cent of men and 46 per cent of women are still alive.
- 15,000 people die in Ireland each year from heart disease;

57 per cent of heart attack victims survive.

• Some 90 per cent of people who have a stroke survive, many are left severely disabled.

The financial confusion caused by serious illness can be even worse than death. With possible loss of income and added expenses such as professional care or house alterations, how would you budget? How would you cope?

With the correct insurance cover, you've protection in the event of the major illnesses of our time, such as heart attack, stroke, cancer, heart surgery, kidney failure, paralysis, permanent disability before the age of 60, major organ transplant, multiple sclerosis, motor neurone disease, brain tumour, loss of speech, severe burns, blindness or coma.

Another option worth looking at for those of us self-employed is Permanent Health Insurance (PHI), which pays out on less 'critical' illnesses and is built into some pension contracts.

Commercial Insurance

Many people operating their business from home are under the mistaken impression that their equipment, tools, etc., are covered under the standard householder's insurance policy. This is not so.

If you wish to be insured in connection with your business you will have to take out a separate commercial insurance policy. Depending on the type of cover required, the premium could range from around £50 to £200 per annum to insure the contents of an office with a word processor, printer, copier, fax, valued at around £20,000.

Unlike a household policy, with commercial insurance you elect what covers you require. You can simply have fire only, 'all risks' cover, or you can select a number of covers within the all risks category, e.g. theft, glass explosion.

If you use your house as an open office/showroom, with people calling for meetings, interviews, to purchase, you could require public liability cover. Depending on the size of risk or the limit of indemnity selected, the premium would be between £150 to £250 per annum.

And, of course, you've all made your wills!

Part II profiles a selection of home-earning entrepreneurs of varying age, socio-economic background and education drawn from both urban and rural locations throughout Ireland.

Part II

Profiles

17

Architects and Artists

Tony and Geraldine O'Daly, Architects

Tony and Geraldine O'Daly Architects are a husband and wife team operating an architectural practice from their home in the south suburbs of Dublin.

Since marrying, Geraldine had always done a certain amount of work from home, as well as part-time research in UCD into the conservation of stonework in historic buildings and monuments. In 1989 Tony left the Office of Public Works so they could set up a joint practice.

Mainly they work on the restoration of old houses, particularly Victorian, as many of their clients are upgrading and extending old buildings. Recently they finished an eighty-three house holiday home scheme in Clifden, County Galway and have also been involved in the design of a thirty-six house holiday home scheme in Hook Head, County Wexford.

'Working from home has been a successful venture,' says Geraldine, 'and the fact that we're both involved in the practice suits our lifestyle.'

Initially a converted bedroom served as office in their own Victorian family house. 'It just wasn't suitable,' says Geraldine. 'One difficulty was clients in the bedroom regions and the other was having three children.' They say the saving factor at the time was their involvement in the holiday home scheme in the West of Ireland, which reduced the number of meetings on their territory.

In 1992 they moved to a three-storey house with a separate entrance to the basement which they converted and refurbished for their office. 'Basically the capital outlay for architects is just a drawing board,' says Geraldine. 'But we have also invested in computers.'

Since the enforcement in June 1992 of the Building Control Act 1990 and the revised Planning Act of 1994, the onus is on architects, rather than as previously on the local authority, to ensure that standards and quality of work conform to existing codes of practice.

'It's complicated and has put additional demands on architects,' says Geraldine. 'Increasingly we need more and more information and with the advances in modern technology, it's now possible to have access to international networks and databases, and for a small annual fee to UCD library's facility for architectural practices.'

'If you can separate your work area from your living quarters, it makes your business more professional and helps your own peace of mind,' says Geraldine. She considers help in the house, 'almost a necessity' and also recommends an independent telephone line and fax, 'mainly to stop the kids answering the phone during office hours.'

Tony and Geraldine see the bonuses of working from home as far outweighing any disadvantages. They have heightened family life and are always available for their children.

Their hours are flexible – Tony, who functions best at night, tends to do a lot of his work then; Geraldine does most of her design work during office hours; they can take the occasional day off, though Geraldine says when she indulges she can feel quite guilt-ridden.

As their practice involves a considerable amount of domestic work, they are accessible to their clients at evenings and weekends. Outside meetings, on-site inspections and liaising with clients prevent any feelings of isolation and they say they can sound off each other.

Pushed to list the disadvantages of working from home, the only one they can come up with is not having as much contact as they would wish with colleagues.

Anne O'Shea and Maurice Noble – Artists

Anne O'Shea and Maurice Noble are an artist couple in their thirties who met at the College of Art & Design in Dublin. They live and work in Skerries with Avril, their two-year-old daughter.

Anne is a painter, working mostly in oils and specialising in portraits. Her portraits are large, varying from four feet to six feet in height. 'I believe that portraits condense people's personalities, emphasise their characteristics and freeze in time their qualities,' she says. 'After seeing the painting this quality materialises into new information, adding to what we already know about the sitter.'

Anne says that she seeks a positive quality in her subject that she projects onto the canvas, using colour to describe it and size to magnify it.

She is involved with the Skerries ARCH group (Association of Recreational Clubs for Handicapped), a social club which meets once a week to play games, dance and talk. One of her commissions was thirty-five portraits of its members to hang in the gym in Fingal Training Centre in Skerries.

Maurice describes himself as, 'a self-taught painter and sculptor, specialising in murals and theatrical masks'. He was involved with Macnas on the dragon of unemployment for the 1994 May Day parade through Dublin and says he finds the idea of giant puppets very exciting. To this end he has worked on several pieces for the Art Squad, a Fingal County Council community employment scheme with which both he and Anne are involved.

He also conducts workshops in mural design, mask making and general arts and crafts with Ronanstown youth services; and he has mounted various productions for Neilstown's teachers group. 'Art is a therapy as well as an occupation, a way of exorcising the demons, of leaving behind a territorial sense and of sharing some of the wonder that is our uniqueness,' he says.

Anne and Maurice share a studio that is a converted bedroom and over the years they have built up their equipment, usually buying what they need between them after 'a well-paid commission'.

'We've been working from home since 1992, a year before Avril was born. Now we choose to to be around her as much as we can. My mother minds her Tuesdays and Thursdays,' says Anne. 'The other days Maurice and I juggle her, our work and the housekeeping and if we're both busy Mum will step in again.'

Anne supplements their income by giving art classes for adults. She only takes enough students to make the venture commercially viable, encourages her pupils to work in the medium of their choice and aims to have them realise their individual potential.

But the backbone of her business and her first love is portrait painting. 'I get a lot of commissions around Christmas, birthdays and for weddings,' she says. 'I really like to meet the person and out of choice have the subject sit for me, but I usually end up working from drawings or photos.'

18

Bird Houses and Teddy Bears

Simone Stephenson – the Birdhouse Company

Simone Stephenson's reasons for turning her back on architecture to design and manufacture bird houses were threefold. When she went shopping for a bird house, she was unable to find one that appealed to her; secondly, she had long planned to set up her own business, though not the obvious architectural practice; and thirdly she wanted to stretch her design skills.

She lives in Dublin and after a detailed look at the existing market and sounding out her idea, she was certain there was a niche to be filled and that her concept was commercially viable.

Her first step was to take a FÁS Business Appraisal Course. During the eleven weeks she learned business methods, how to assess the market, carry out market research, etc. On the last day she produced her first prototype.

Next she applied for and was accepted by Forbairt for a feasibility study grant. She also got a place in the Enterprise

Development Programme run by the Dublin Institute of Technology. This is a start your own business support scheme aimed at entrepreneurial graduates in the twenty-five to thirty-five age group. By now she had set up an office at home and did not need to avail of the centre's office space and phone, fax and computer facilities.

Then came the legwork to find the right wood and colour. 'I went around timber suppliers – I knew some of them from my architectural work and got more out of the *Golden Pages.* I collected wood samples and did test stains until I got the right effect.' She settled on weather resistant birch plywood and Medex, exterior grade mdf (medium density fibreboard).

After looking at several firms, Simone chose a Dublin-based company to manufacture the bird houses to her design and specification. Approximately a hundred units are made up at a time.

Production began in November 1993. Within the first eighteen months in excess of 800 units were manufactured, over 40 per cent going for export, mainly to Germany, Switzerland and the UK.

Again, Simone says, she put in further legwork and lots of networking with regard to distribution. She showed at trade fairs, which opened both retail and private doors, and went around shops who initially took the bird houses only on a sale or return basis.

Retail outlets in Dublin include Brown Thomas, Presents of Mind and Enclosures in Blackrock. The bird houses are on permanent display in the Dublin headquarters of the Craft Council of Ireland.

The administrative end of The Birdhouse Company is well

organised. 'I keep the paperwork manageable. The accounts are on computer, which I update regularly, and I have an accountant. She employs on a part-time basis for assembly and packing, deals direct with an increasing amount of customers, and operates a mail order facility.

The innovative designs and colour schemes of her bird houses have fired public and media imagination and she says she has received a lot of publicity – magazine and newspaper features, appearances on the *Late Late Show* and *Live at Three*, all of which she recognises as being, 'good for business'.

The main difficulties she has encountered are the escalation in price of both material and production and reliance on others. 'In some cases with the rising prices it can be difficult to get new customers and indeed to keep old ones. If I had more volume production costs could be reduced and it would be more economical all around,' she says. 'Also you've to learn patience when you're relying on other people to produce work on time. But occasionally, it's no harm to give them a push.'

Joan Hanna, Craft T-Bear

Trading under the label Craft T-Bear, Cork-based Joan Hanna was the first person in Ireland to make jointed teddy bears aimed specifically at adult collectors. In happier times for them, while holidaying in Ireland, Mia Farrow and Woody Allen were two of her initial customers when she started in 1989.

Joan has been interested in soft toys since she was a

teenager. 'Despite being advised by a "business expert" to go for jewellery rather than bears, which he said wouldn't be commercial, I went ahead with Craft T-Bear, determined to prove that an international market did exist for a good quality collectors' bear,' says Joan, delighted to have scored over and over again.

Bears have become big business worldwide, particularly in Japan. In December 1994 Teddygirl broke all records by selling to a Japanese collector in Christies of London for £110,000.

'To date I have made over a thousand bears. The expansion of my business has been gradual, keeping pace with the growing interest and international demand for bears,' says Joan. Craft T-Bears retail in Memoir of Dublin, Nostalgia of Kenmare, Yesterdays of Cork and Kilkenny, and Teddy Bears of Whitney, Oxfordshire, though at least 90 per cent end up outside Ireland.

The bears are made from mohair, distressed for an aged look. The most popular colours are traditional or antique gold. The stuffing is polyester, wood wool or PVC pellets; paws are suede, suedette or wool felt and eyes are glass. Nose, mouth and claws are hand stitched. The largest, at twenty-three inches, is priced around £254 and the smallest, a mere eight inches, costs about £25.

Joan travels regularly to the UK for teddy bear fairs, advertises in the *Teddy Bear Guide,* circulated as far afield as Singapore, Australia and New Zealand; and does mail order. She is commissioned by the Keystone Traders, a group of Americans who tour Britain each year collecting bears, to make their official souvenir bear.

One of her bears features in Pauline Cockrill's *Teddy Bear Encyclopaedia* – the definitive reference book for arctophiles. She is also founder of Bear Friends, a friendship club for people in Ireland who collect bears. 'At the group's first meeting in the Westbury Hotel, the management entered into the spirit of the occasion by providing bowls of porridge for the bears,' she says.

Start up costs for Craft T-Bear were low. Joan operates out of a spare bedroom and her equipment comprises two domestic sewing machines and an overlocker, used specifically for bear clothes. In the beginning she bought only small amounts of mohair, which varies in price from £30 to £80 a metre. Nowadays she buys in bulk, sourcing in Yorkshire or Germany.

'I prefer to work mornings only, but sometimes in peak periods and to fill orders I've to put in another stint during the day, though the amount of time I can spend at one sitting is limited, as my neck gives me trouble,' she says. 'It takes approximately five hours to make a bear – stuffing the head with wool alone can take up to two hours.'

Administrative work is minimal and book-keeping she has simplified to expenditure out, monies in, keeping all receipts and having the books audited at the year end.

Joan's limited edition of three Irish bears has proved an international success. The Aran bear wears an Aran sweater, tweed trousers and carries a currach made by Flan Egan of Clifden. The Achill Island bear has a grandfather shirt, tweed waistcoat, chord breeches and holds a minature turf creel. Peig, based on Peig Sayers of the Blasket Islands, is dressed from photographs in a skirt, apron and tweed jacket.

19

Cakes and Catering

Jill Aston – Cake Craft

Cake Craft specialises in theme cakes for corporate and personal clients. The County Dublin based business, brainchild of Jill Aston, took off initially by word of mouth. Over the years she has consolidated by selected advertising and mail shots.

As well as regular orders from PR companies and advertising agencies for product replicas and company logos, Jill has made cakes for outlets such as Ardmore Studios, RTE, Tennants Lager, The Point, Nokia and Lillie's Bordello nightclub.

She supplies exclusively to Quinnsworth in the Merrion Centre, Dublin and delivers there as a collection point for orders. In 1991 she held a two-day edible art exhibition in conjunction with an appearance on *Kenny Live.*

Some of her most interesting commissions include 463 individual rugby shirt cakes for the Golden Oldies rugby dinner; a piano accordian cake, measuring three feet by two and a half feet; The Edge's car; forty cakes in the shape of a bottle to mark the launch of Sheridan's liqueur and three 'drill' cakes for Black and Decker.

It all began when the cakes she made for her own children's parties led to orders for other children's parties. Then on the spur of the moment, a few days before Mother's Day in 1987, she made up two samples – a figure in a bath and a basket of fresh flowers – drove around to friends' houses and within three days had orders for twenty cakes.

The benefits of working from home Jill lists as: being available for her three children; no payment for childcare; choice of working hours and, 'Very importantly,' she says, 'working from home gives me the space to be creative.'

To make cakes commercially she needed a second kitchen. She approached the health board, had a visit from the environmental health officer and applied to the IDA for a grant. By this stage, she says, she had the start of an impressive client list and confidence in the viability of her product.

After much perseverance she received her grant, not for the actual cakes, but for their artwork. 'It was a small employment grant paid in two parts, a wage while I was starting up the business, but I put it towards installing the new kitchen.' In keeping with EC regulations, the kitchen is tiled from floor to ceiling, has a double sink, a fan over the oven and a stainless steel table.

Jill considers the organisational end as important as the creative side of Cake Craft. Sponges are supplied by a local baker who makes to her recipe; icing and colourings are delivered as required and cake boards were sourced in Galway.

'I work better under pressure, meeting deadlines. In the beginning I found it difficult to sell either myself or my product, mainly, I think, because the public perception of a cake is a round shape with a cherry on top. Gradually that has changed, though not before I'd almost exhausted the dictionary looking for alternative words for cake!'

Clients are encouraged to come up with their own ideas and Jill says she takes great pleasure in executing them. 'When I first started, I knew there was a market for my product and I was right, but I had no idea working up the business to its present state would be such a challenge, though I've had enormous support from the major bakeries and great help from friends.'

She keeps a graph of quarterly averages and annual sales; predicts peak turnover periods; analyses when to make up new samples; proportions prices and equates raw material costs.

'Cake Craft is much more than making cakes – it's about doing the books, banking, ordering, getting in money – all the attendant administration that goes with running a business, plus a large amount of time talking to clients on the phone,' she says. 'And over the years, I'm pleased to say I've become a lot braver about chasing up agreed invoices.'

Maher family – Boyton Catering

The Maher family, Don, Jo, and their daughters Margaret and Patricia are all involved in Boyton Catering, the family business which has been operating from their home in south county Dublin since 1972.

Like many a successful operation, Boyton's potential was identified, evolved and grew to fill a gap in an existing market. Jo, who had nursed her mother through a terminal illness, filled the void after her death by supplying cakes to a local delicatessen. The popularity of her cakes and increasing orders were the triggers on which their business was founded.

Over the past two decades the company has developed to suit changing market trends, different lifestyles and varying tastes. 'We've never advertised,' says Don. 'We didn't have to. Our business has always been repeat, referral and by word of mouth.'

The Mahers will cater for virtually any function from corporate affairs to weddings and funerals. 'We'll take the hassle out of cocktail dos, dinner parties and buffet occasions,' says Don. Preferred numbers for catering are in the 20 to 200 range.

Currently what the Mahers categorise as 'high class take away food' for private entertaining accounts for approximately half their turnover. 'The nature of entertaining and the pattern of food has changed over the years, with take away becoming very popular,' he says.

While people are entertaining as much as ever in their homes, the format has become more informal. Unlike a decade ago, it's usually only for special occasions that Boyton is called in to cater from start to finish. According to Don, 'What's increasingly occurring is that we're asked to supply the food, crockery, cutlery, glassware and table linen along with one of our trained freelancers who'll serve and wash up.'

'The trend in food is steering away from red meats. Fish is popular, but it's also expensive,' says Don. 'There's a move back towards good quality traditional home cooking, which is what we've based our reputation on. Would-be clients who call here are welcome to see us in operation.'

In Boyton Catering's current brochure, there are at least thirty starters to choose from including smoked salmon parcels, warm salads and a variety of soups; main courses, such as medallion of beef in Irish Mist, breast of chicken in champagne or crown roast of lamb can be followed by a choice of more than fifty desserts.

Outside the family, the company employs seven people on a permanent basis and out-reach worker numbers vary with the demands and seasonality of the business. From its inception the business has been financially self-sufficient and never received grant aid.

The Mahers' background is firmly rooted in the catering/ hotel industry. Don's family owned the Boyton Hotel in Thurles (now Hayes's Hotel) and he took a management training course in Jurys Hotel. Jo did hotel management in the College of Catering in Cathal Brugha Street, Dublin and was catering supervisor in the Gresham Hotel. Their son David, still a student and daughters Patricia and Margaret all took hotel management. Their two sons-in-law are also in the catering business – though not with Boyton!

To survive in an increasingly competitive market, quality, organisation and efficiency are the company keywords. While each family member has a working knowledge of the different aspects of the business, they have their areas of specialisation. Don's is ordering and general organisation;

Jo is the expert in desserts, Patricia handles functions and Margaret does the accounts.

The family sees the advantages of working from home as far outweighing the disadvantages. The benefits they list are financial and in the quality of life. 'Because overheads are minimal, we can keep costings within reason and we don't have to commute,' says Don. 'The downside is the unsociable lifestyle. We're cocooned and if it weren't for the functions we cater, it would be all too easy to lose touch with the real world.'

20

Candles and Cloona

Ciaran Ganter – Candlewood

'I'd always been interested in candles both as an art form and from a practical point of view. From keeping my eyes open and asking around, I discovered a gap in the market,' says Ciaran Ganter, owner of Dublin-based company Candlewood, which claims to be one of the few in Ireland specialising in the manufacture of top quality beeswax candles.

Of a more practical than academic disposition, Ciaran wanted to leave school from an early age but, bowing to parental pressure, he stayed on until the end of Christmas term in sixth year. While still in school, he took an evening course in wood turning. It was with wood that he made his commercial debut. Using beech and yew, he turned bowls, clocks, lamps, bud vases and ashtrays which he polished with beeswax and sold in local markets.

But he discovered that his products were exclusive rather than mass market and for them to be commercially viable his prices would have to be higher than feasible. His clocks proved particularly popular and he filled some private commissions, before deciding to specialise in candles.

Start up costs were in the region of £5,000. He received funding and a mentor from his local enterprise board. 'The banks were very helpful too, but then I believe small businesses are the thing of the future and there are a lot of incentives around to give people a start.'

He imports most of his raw materials. The beeswax he buys in 100 lb weights. Because he works from home, production costs are pared and he hopes by keeping his selling price down that he'll interest more people in his product. 'Then, as demand grows, I can go for more commercially realistic prices.'

'When working out costings, I don't take into account the phone, ESB, fuel, car insurance or personal expenditure. I make only a nominal contribution towards living expenses and haven't to pay rent at a commercial rate,' he says.

Ciaran handles all aspects of the business himself from the making, marketing and selling to administration. He works daily from nine to five and longer when manu-facturing; then he keeps going until the wax runs out. In lull periods he manufactures and sells beeswax polish.

'I'm highly motivated, work hard, believe in and love what I'm doing, but it can be lonely. I've always liked being with people.' As a member of the Woodturners Guild, he attends meetings regularly, particularly enjoying the social aspect.

Peak manufacturing time is September onwards for the Christmas trade. Candlewood's outlets include the Irish Life Mall, IDA Enterprise Centre in Pearse Street and the

Blackrock Market. Ciaran has also taken a stand at the Brighter Homes Exhibiton in the RDS.

Looking ahead, he predicts an increasing emphasis on craft orientated industry. 'My ambition is to own a gallery craft shop outside of Dublin where I'd be dealing with people and they'd be able to watch the manufacturing processes.' Ultimately he reckons he'll diversify, but always 'sticking to the natural'.

Dhara Kelly and Emer Gaffney – Cloona Health Centre

Cloona Health Centre in County Mayo, the first health farm in Ireland, was started in the 1970s by Ceylon-born Sonia Kelly. Two decades later it is run by her son Dhara and his wife Emer Gaffney in a harmonious partnership that they say owes much to planning and time-tabling.

Dhara handles the administration and functions as general co-ordinator. Emer who is ITEC qualified, is a reflexologist, yoga teacher and masseuse.

Cloona, a converted woollen mill, lies in the shadow of Croagh Patrick on the south side of Clew Bay. It is situated in rural seclusion three miles outside Westport. 'The personal aspect of this business is very important,' says Dhara. 'The fact that we the owners are also the operators and that we're a family makes for a bonding between the guests and ourselves.' He also considers it 'invaluable' that their living accommodation is in the grounds, but separate from the Centre.

Since the birth of their two children, Dhara and Emer have

to be even more organised. 'It's tricky,' he says. 'We've no home help and, as we don't involve our children in the centre, we've to alternate our presence in the home, so basically when Emer is there I'm here and vice versa.'

They have rescheduled operations to maximise on time.

Morning yoga has been brought forward by a quarter of an hour, with Emer serving lunch to their guests on her own. This allows them to extend their own break by fifteen minutes which, Dhara says, reduces pressure and gives them a leisurely lunch.

'Flexibility is most important and if our workload wasn't interchangeable, we couldn't operate,' says Dhara. 'We're both competent to carry out all the tasks involved in running the centre, with the exception that I don't do the therapies, such as massage or reflexology.'

Dhara handles the shopping and organises food and menus. 'Since we've had the children, I've had to become more methodical. Previously, some days I'd be in town five times, other days twice. That doesn't happen any more. It can't. I now do the shopping three days a week and early in the morning.'

As well as food for the planned menus, there's the post office, bank and the various other paraphernalia associated with administration. Dhara keeps accounts up to date himself, but also employs an accountant.

Cloona is an operation that of necessity has always had to be self supporting. 'From the day it was founded, we didn't seem to fall into any of the categories for grant aid and so we've never got any money from anywhere at any time,' says Dhara.

They advertise intermittently, more previously than recently, but consider that long term it has paid off. Business is up to 50 per cent repeat, with some guests returning two to three times a year. 'Word of mouth is most effective in our line of business. We rarely come across anyone who has only seen an ad or the *Golden Pages*,' says Dhara.

Cloona opens from March to November, with a Sunday to Saturday programme to facilitate registration and housekeeping. Dhara and Emer take only single bookings, as years of experience have proved that there is more commitment from people on their own. Total, not partial, participation in the programme of activities is expected.

21

Computer People

Regina McGarrigle – Mayo Editorial Services

Regina McGarrigle, owner of Mayo Editorial Services, is a freelance teleworker, living and working from her home in Castlebar. She provides a scientific and technical editing service, proofreading and conference editing facilities. She also has a home page on the Internet's World Wide Web and offers a WWW authoring service.

She graduated from UCD in 1975 with a science degree and an unfulfilled love of words. 'I'd always loved words and the organisation of them, and I was good at putting together reports.'

She did part-time teaching in UCD's biochemistry department and some tutorial work until a newspaper ad proved her lucky break. Elsevier, specialising in the publication of scientific, technological and medical subjects, was in the market for a freelance proofreader/copy editor with a scientific background.

During the 1980s copy was still edited on paper, sent out

to the typesetter, returned and checked. Regina kept her finger on the pulse of the freelance editing market while her children were small – she has six. When her eldest started college she returned to work full-time.

'After some preliminary market research I found there was a demand for qualified freelance editors. I had no problem lining up clients – I just approached international publishing houses who specialise in science,' she says.

It was the beginning of the 1990s. The words 'teleworking' and 'telecottaging' had been coined. The opportunities, potential and benefits of teleworking were receiving international recognition.

It was a growth industry, with an ever increasing demand for skilled workers, a kiss of life for job creation in rural communities, a support for small businesses, an opportunity for access to new technology. It was ideal for the self-employed; perfect for operating from home, though, for the more gregarious, telecottaging, using local centres equipped with modern technology where a group of people could work, was an equally viable option.

Some of the publishing houses Regina dealt with were beginning to edit solely on disk. Teleworking beckoned. She invested in a computer, carried out further market research, discovered openings for scanning, editing and producing camera ready copy. She applied for and received in the region of £2,500 EC Leader funding for expansion.

'I was now a teleworker with an electonic cottage, complete with scanners, e-mail, fax, computer and laser printer. I use all of these media plus couriers to send and receive manuscripts from all over the world.' About 75 per cent of her work still comes in hard copy and the majority of those who send disks follow up with hard copy. 'This is the way it'll be until ISDN (Integrated Services Digital Network) for data transfer becomes more standard, which will also be great for teleconferencing.'

'I no longer have to chase work, people come to me; I've a lot of repeats and edit certain journals on a regular basis,' she says. In the region of 50 per cent of her work is from publishing houses; most of the remainder being made up of technical reports for organisations in the scientific, biomedical and environmental fields. The conference service, which she supplies and considers an expanding market, involves editing speakers' papers up to supplying camera ready professional copy either on paper or disk.

Regina's office, at the back of her garage converted courtesy of Leader funding, is custom designed for ease of working and to meet her requirements. She is at her best early in the morning; tries to keep her working day to eight hours and to operate as far ahead as possible, but says she rarely succeeds on either count, as her workload is constantly on the increase.

She charges her clients hourly rates, keeps a notebook on her desk and is punctilious about logging time.

'When you work from home your standards are expected to be higher than those of your counterparts in full-time publishing. It's a constant challenge and keeps you on your toes, knowing you're only as good as your last job.'

Despite the bad press teleworking has acquired in some quarters for psychological deprivation due to lack of human contact, Regina has no sensation of isolation. 'It's the kind of work you need to carry out without interruption and to give your whole attention to.' She is active in Telecottages Ireland and says the members look out for and support each other. There is also time spent meeting clients and attending functions.

She has no outside help in the house, but is organised, shopping once a week, laying out menus in advance and using the weekends for forward planning. 'When you're working from home you need a huge amount of back up and support from partners and family. I couldn't cope without their help. Everyone does a bit and we manage well.'

Tony O'Connell – Channel-One

From childhood Tony O'Connell dreamt of owning his own business. His ambition was realised with the setting up of Channel-One, his electronic shopping mall.

While in college he became involved in network marketing with a UK operation and he was bitten by the selling bug. He attended seminars and workshops both in Ireland and the UK, learned to make product presentations and to present himself in a commercial way.

After graduating from Portobello College in 1994 with a BA Hons in Marketing, he and a friend came up with the concept of the mobile office – a laptop (notebook) computer, complete with fax facility and modem and a mobile phone packed into a briefcase. The joint project died when his partner moved to County Clare, but still set on the idea Tony pursued it, sourcing his product in Galway. 'Because I wasn't an expert in computing I wanted to work with a company that was.'

During this time he became aware of the growth in the United States of shopping on Internet and considered the time was ripe in Ireland to sell computer equipment and supplies via Internet.

The pioneering aspect and mobility particularly appealed to Tony. Preliminary market research added to his optimism and the calls he made on suppliers were positive.

He spent a few weeks at home in Galway putting together a business proposal, arranged funding to the amount of £10,000, of which £4,000 was allocated for research and development (R and D) and returned to Dublin, where he took a lease on an apartment in the Temple Bar area to function as office and living accommodation.

An annual subscription of £150 accessed him to Ireland On Line Internet, which also links to the international information superhighway and e-mail, with 24-hour service seven days a week. His database is accessible worldwide to 30 million people to browse his shopping mall, place orders by credit card and be guaranteed delivery within 24 hours. A mobile phone gives Tony further access to his clients.

'I love being part of an electronic community,' he says with enthusiasm, though he does admit to feelings of loneliness and isolation, which he has counteracted by the acquisition of Elvis, an extrovert guinea pig.

'There's always the fear of failure and it's difficult not having somebody to sound off ideas with. But when you're self-employed, while it's hard and the hours are long, you've freedom, control over your life and the option to make a lot of money. This is a business that can be operated from anywhere in the world,' he says.

He considers he has got in at ground floor level, predicting Ireland's business future being closely allied with Internet which he says has taken off under its own momentum. 'It's ideal for purchasing, sales and marketing and environmental scanning.'

Patrick Quilligan – Mobile Computer Work Station

When freelance journalist Patrick Quilligan got his first computer, he went to buy a mobile work station. He discovered that what was available was imported and expensive. Nothing daunted, he designed one to meet his specific requirements, using the criteria of compactness, mobility and high finish. He built the prototype at home.

Certain he had a commercially viable product, he felt that production was the next step. After a quick scout around for funding, he settled on using his own resources. 'I'm not a very bureaucratic type of person. If funds are available and can be got at quickly, fine,' says Patrick. 'But I don't find endless obstacles conducive to business.'

He approached several cabinet makers. 'It was a long drawn out process before I found the right person. I had to shop around for someone who would be *au fait* with the product, efficient, enthusiastic, able to iron out problems, and whose price was right.'

Patrick sourced the hardware himself – MDF (micro density fibreboard) – 18 mm, and for the top of the desk 25 mm to accommodate a heavy monitor; brackets for the side flaps from Germany (the fourth type that he sourced); four castors per unit; rollers for the keyboard and printing shelves; an aluminium handle at the back and a black satin finish. He gets twenty work stations made up at a time, which come assembled, not flat packed.

The stations are on view in selected ESB Shop Electric branches. He advertises in appropriate papers and magazines and displays at shows in the RDS, such as the Brighter Homes Exhibiton and at various computer shows. Before going on the *Late Late*'s Enterprise Show, which he says was a very good shopfront, he took out a patent.

While subscribing to the theory that getting there is more exciting than arriving, Patrick has pride and belief in his product. 'It's Irish, of high quality and keeping money circulating in this country. As it achieves more market penetration, the sales curve is on the increase. It's an aesthetic as well as a functional piece, and because of its compactness and mobility, ideal for small apartments.'

22

Marketing

Marie Cooney – Tipperary Natural Mineral Water Company

Tipperary Natural Mineral Water was founded in 1986 by accountant brothers Patrick and Nicholas Cooney and Marie, Patrick's wife.

The family's original business, based in Borrisoleigh in County Tipperary, was a wholesale distribution company for packaged beers. As part of an expansion plan they diversified into soft drinks in the late 1970s. After a few years the village water supply was no longer sufficient to meet the growing requirements of the business.

A local diviner discovered a new source of water at a depth of 320 feet, which after analysis proved to be of exceptional quality. It was the 1980s: natural mineral water had become an 'in' drink and the Cooneys recognised and grasped the market opportunity.

The name Tipperary owes its origins to a cruise on the Nile. 'On the last evening out the captain requested members of the various nationalities to do a party piece,' says Marie. 'The Irish group sang, "It's a Long Way to Tipperary". Everyone seemed to know the song and they all joined in the chorus. People from Japan, Australia, America and at least ten other countries. We just couldn't pass up on the opportunity of using an internationally recognised name for our mineral water.'

Marie handles the marketing and PR from her home-based office and is all in favour of working from home. 'As well as being my own boss and having freedom, I can maximise time and operate more efficiently than if I were commuting. I've everything to hand here – two telephone lines, fax, answering machine, and I'm linked directly to the office for communication purposes and secretarial requirements.'

Her first foray into the marketing of Tipperary was a trade fair in Scotland, shortly after the birth of her fourth child – she subsequently has had a fifth. 'I just followed my nose and it went well.'

The next hurdle was to break into Dublin's restaurant and hotel trade – the pubs were being looked after by the wholesale end of the business. 'I started at the top of Grafton Street, with my bottle of Tipperary in my briefcase and I went up one side and down the other. I worked the city and outskirts like that. It was difficult. Other waters were already well established and an order was a big treat,' says Marie.

Despite lack of formal training – she had previously worked in banking and publishing – she became increasingly involved in public relations which, she says, has played an enormous part in building the Tipperary brand. 'I had an instinctive awareness and knowledge, a firm belief in my product and I like people.'

Stepping stones over the years include product placements on various television programmes; and Pat and Marie's appearance on the *Late Late Show*; redesign of the bottle plus minimalist labeling which helped to double sales within a year; gold medal awards for excellence from the British Bottlers Institute; and being the first Irish water to gain EC recognised natural mineral water status.

Diversification under the Tipperary brand name includes a cosmetic kit pack for first-class passengers for several airlines, also the redesign of a facial spray for the pharmaceutical industry. Tipperary is also distributed in twenty-litre office coolers throughout Ireland and is brand leader in this sector. 'The beauty of all this is that you're keeping the name to the forefront,' says Marie.

As the company has grown, a greater amount of Marie's time is spent away from her desk at meetings, networking, visiting hotels and restaurants and negotiating deals. Increasingly the administrative side of her career is blurring with the 'social' aspect of sponsorships, national and international shows and trade fairs, an escalating amount of travel and evening functions.

She says, 'But it's working and it's worth it. A decade on we're exporting to fifteen countries, including the States, Japan, Malta, the Middle East and mainland Europe.'

While Marie says she never stops thinking, planning and looking at markets, keeping the fabric and balance of family life intact is of equal importance to her. On the return journey from bringing the younger children to school in the mornings, she collects her housekeeper, 'who keeps the household ticking over and without whom my career would not be possible.'

23

Ostriches and Tourism

Brian Purcell – Ostrich Farmer

'Ostrich farming appeals right across the board,' says Brian Purcell, the County Meath cattle farmer who brought ostrich farming to Ireland in 1994. 'It's commercially viable, with good growth potential and is suitable for people with a few spare acres, farmers who want to diversify and as an investment opportunity.'

The ostriches which are imported from the UK, where they've been climatised, originate mainly from Namibia, Botswana, Zimbabwe and Israel. Within a year of Brian bringing in the first ostrich more than 200 people in Ireland were involved in ostrich farming. 'It's not physically hard work, but it is time intensive and does require a certain amount of know how,' says Brian. 'Two acres can accomodate up to twenty head. High fencing and access to shelter are necessary.'

It costs about £2,000 for a three-month male and female, each weighing in at about the size of a turkey. A breeding unit is frequently formed of one male and two females, the male becoming productive at around three years of age and the female at two.

'Though initial costs appear high, as with any other form of breeding, good stock does not come cheap,' says Brian. 'It's not a bad investment when you consider ostriches live for about seventy years and breed for an average of twenty-five. Presuming a female produces twenty-three chicks annually, if they survive, return can be in the region of £11,500 per annum or £230,000 over 20 years.'

Once ostriches reach twelve months they're regarded as being relatively resistant to extremes of temperatures and wetness, important considerations with the Irish climate. They feed like other fowl, grazing on grass and gravel, and require a kilo a day of patented food. Full grown they're about eight feet tall and can run at speeds of up to forty miles per hour.

Ostriches have the reputation of being bad tempered and quick to nip. 'They enjoy human contact,' defends Brian, who is also enthusiastic about their different personalities, saying some are consistently good humoured, and others quite moody. 'One of the loveliest sights is to watch a flock of them dancing in the field.'

The options with ostrich farming are breeding or slaughter. Brian Purcell considers slaughter the most viable. 'You've only to wait twelve months and purely because of the laws of supply and demand, ostrich meat is regarded as a delicacy. I forsee real demand in a few years' time among top restaurateurs.'

Annually ostriches lay approximately forty-five eggs, each

weighing in the region of 1.5 kilos. (Interestingly, laying time is usually around four o'clock in the afternoon.) Eggs are incubated at controlled temperatures for about forty-two days. The bad news for breeders is that not every egg hatches out and of those that do often only about a third reach the three-months stage when the chicks are regarded as survivors.

Incubation facilities are provided for Brian Purcell's clients through Pat McKenna from Balrothery, North County Dublin.

Joking that he doesn't 'want to put all his eggs in one basket', Pat runs two 120-egg incubators. The process is highly scientific, with eggs being 'candled' every fortnight and regular contact is maintained with UK embryologist, Dr Charles Deeming.

Another string for development in Brian's bow is egg craft, the painting and carving of eggs, regarded among some connoisseurs as a collectible art form. The feathers he sells to Dublin's Gate Theatre for costume trimming.

The world's first ostrich abattoir was constructed in South Africa in the 1960s for fresh meat and, because of world demand at the time, ostrich skin leather. Brian Purcell has plans to build the first one in Ireland.

Gubbins family – Dunkerron Guest House and Rent-an-Irish Cottage

In 1988 Brian Gubbins and four partners purchased Dunkerron, a nineteenth-century Victorian house sited on a seventy-acre parkland estate bordering Kenmare Bay on the

Ring of Kerry. Three years later he bought out his partners and since then Dunkerron has become both the family home and roots of the Gubbins' expanding tourism-related business. Brian's wife Moya, solicitor daughter (also Moya) and son J. C. are all involved.

The family also has a 50 per cent stake in sixty-seven Rent-an-Irish Cottage units in seven different locations throughout the West of Ireland and an estate agency in Limerick city, which also serves as a business administrative base.

They learnt their business from the ground up. 'We had to. When we started we didn't understand the intricacies of tourism,' says J. C. Gubbins who, since finishing college in 1992, has made it his career. Until then, Trimark, a Dublin-based marketing company in which the family held a substantial interest, marketed and managed their holiday home locations. Now all reservations are handled internally.

Located in one of the most beautiful and historical parts of County Kerry, the ten-bedroomed Dunkerron (subsequently extended to fourteen bedrooms) came with twenty self-catering cottages which were in relatively good condition, but the house required extensive refurbishment, which to cost price ratio is reckoned at 50/50.

'We haven't seriously marketed the guest house,' says J. C. 'We get a lot of repeat business during the high season, mainly due to my mother's popularity as a hostess and some tight management practices, but a focused marketing strategy would increase off season occupancy.'

'My mother loves it, but it's hard work,' says J. C. 'It's too small to employ a good manager and getting too big to run herself.' Dunkerron is tied in with various Bord Fáilte agencies and listed in the national guest house guide. The family are considering alternatives, such as Elegant Ireland, an organisation which rents out on a self-catering basis houses of Dunkerron calibre.

Tourism is a labour-intensive industry, much of it seasonal and part time. During high season the Gubbins employ in the region of thirty people for Rent-an-Irish Cottage and ten in Dunkerron, phasing down to around a total of twenty at off-peak times. Staff includes supervisors, cleaners, administrators, chef, and maintenance men such as thatchers, electricians, plumbers, decorators.

'One of the pluses of a family run business is that we share successes and in times of crisis, you know you'll be supported.' Of necessity, J. C. Gubbins says, it's a hands-on operation – with each member of the family knowing the different aspects of the business and being capable of standing in for each other when necessary.'

'It's much more than a weekly wage,' says J. C. 'It's ours, so we work harder to give it our best and hopefully reap the benefits in the long term. We've more security than others because we look after it ourselves and know exactly what's going on.'

The family says that since they started working together, while they've become much closer, at times still they can be too casual with each other. On the downside they cite lack of privacy with people constantly in their home.

The Gubbinses believe it takes five years to turn a business around. When they took over Dunkerron and Rent-an-Irish Cottage, they cut expenses to the bone and, as turnover increased they spent on refurbishment. In 1994 Dunkerron guest house and cottages topped 2,000 bed nights each and Rent-an-Irish Cottage 9,750.

'We've good ideas about where we want to bring the business. But it's only since we've put the "lean years" behind us that we're in a position to do so,' says J. C., for whom the most exciting aspects of the business are developing and tapping into new markets, meeting and ensuring guests' satisfaction and creating added value.

24

Pottery and Tapestry

Dave Dain – Potter

Dave Dain lives in the Comeragh Mountains in County Waterford. He has been earning his living as a potter since 1985.

When he returned to Dublin in the 1970s after a few years of teaching English in Spain, he became involved in school supplies, got an agency for pottery supplies, and became interested in pottery. 'I didn't like Dublin and I decided very naïvely that I'd be able to earn a living in the country from pottery within a year.'

He rented a cottage in County Clare and twelve months later he had used up his savings and shed his romantic notions. After moving to County Waterford, where he did a variety of jobs to make a living, he seriously started into pottery.

Learning as he went, he built a wheel in a week from the gear box of a Volkswagon Beetle – the commercial price is about £900. It cost Dave £3. And that was for a welder to cut a piece of metal. He constructed the kiln that operates with waste oil from scratch and only recently bought an electric one. He taught himself to make pots, then to fire, glaze and find markets.

'Pottery can be approached with just a lump of clay, a good pair of hands and a kiln. But it's not easy,' he says. 'The way I went about it was difficult, but it has given me a better understanding than if I'd gone to a college or a working pottery. Mine is the holistic approach: I was my own teacher and I try to have my pupils do the same.'

Gradually Dave acquired a reputation and began to build up an income from selling at field days, exhibitions, and with sales and classes from home. 'Bit by bit it fell into place and making saleable items was a great cause for celebration.'

Then children from around the area began coming to his home to make pots. A speech therapist with a school in Cashel that caters for special needs saw the children at work and realised how beneficial pottery would be on their school curriculum.

Dave went to the school one day a week for five years and it was a successful experiment. 'Clay is a great therapy. A lump of it can be used to symbolise something bad from childhood. After squashing and kneading it, you feel much better,' he says. 'The pottery was very basic and the quality of pots wasn't great, but it got the pupils talking and relating and they enjoyed it.'

Dave finds there is most demand for domestic ware, flower pots and patio pots. He uses the mug as a yardstick. 'It's my basic currency. It's a good seller, because it's functional and relatively cheap.' However, he says, outletting through shops can be a problem as pottery is a relatively slow mover and, with a mark-up of as much as 100 per cent, it works out expensive.

'When you start making pottery, you're influenced by other potters, but eventually your own style emerges.' He has never lost the thrill of creating and says, 'When you've used a new glaze, it's exciting – like unwrapping a present at Christmas – to open the door of the kiln and find it has worked well.'

In 1993 Dave became involved in the Cluain Training and Enterprise Centre in Clonmel, which was set up for young adults marginalised from society because of psychological problems.

With a referral from NRB (National Rehabilitation Board) and funding from Europe, the Centre looked at various options that would enable the trainees to develop personal and life skills with a work-orientated programme to facilitate their progress from sheltered to open employment and, if desired, with further training to self-employment in three to five years.

Modules of desk-top publishing, catering and pottery were settled on. 'The trainees themselves, many of them highly intelligent, wanted another crack at life,' says Dave. 'From the start we determined not to go down the path of boredom of many similar centres.'

Dave handled pottery. The catering was tied up with CERT and DTP with City and Guilds. 'Originally it was planned that pottery would be less of a discipline than the others. But it took off beyond all expectations and was soon heading towards a commercial standard. We don't do any spoon feeding. We get the trainees to take responsibility for their attendance and their own work.'

'Despite the isolation of where I live, people still come to buy pots. I'm glad I did pottery and I enjoy working with my hands. The income is relatively low compared to other jobs. If I had a wife and children I'd have to work much harder.' He says he gets a lot of job satisfaction, particularly counting the money after a field day!

Angela Forte – Tapestry Artist

Tapestry artist Angela Forte has been working from home since 1987. Her introduction to tapestry in school was love at first sight, and when she went to the National College of Art and Design (NCAD) predictably, she specialised in woven textiles.

After graduation she took the Crafts Council business training course, which she found invaluable. 'When you finish college you haven't an idea about administration or how to run a craft studio.'

In 1983 she set up in the IDA Enterprise Centre in Pearse Street, grant aided for five years for equipment and rent. 'It all fell into place and was perfectly timed. Finding good studio space surrounded by other craft people can be very difficult,' she says.

While doing the business course, Angela had discovered a commercially viable market for eighteen inch by twenty inch landscape wall hangings for outletting in selected craft shops in Ireland and the United States. She bought traditional floor looms in Finland and set about developing the business, while at the same time pursuing commissions for large scale tapestries.

The venture was successful, so much so that Angela had to employ an apprentice. 'I worked like mad, doing a lot of promotions and demonstrations. It was a conscious decision, to get my name known and it stood to me,' says Angela. 'But I became torn between the commercial and the creative. In the end the creative won.'

That she married around the same time as she moved her studio to home in Dublin's northside, she assures, had nothing to do with her decision to work from home. Since the birth of her daughter in 1992, she says working at home has allowed her the flexibility and freedom to be both a tapestry artist and a mother.

'Every piece I do is a stepping stone, some, such as the Birth of Two Selves, commissioned by The National Maternity Hospital for their centenary year, stands out as a major landmark. I am making a decent living and growing creatively.'

'When I'm working I need concentrated time, solitude and little disturbance. Operating from home facilitates conducive conditions and when you've children, if you wish, you can cut back on work,' says Angela. 'The middle of the 1990s has been particularly creative. I function at a slower pace and yet I get a lot more work done in a given time.'

Angela says she is not house proud, but when she is in the studio from nine to six, she employs someone to handle basic domestic chores. 'I'm disturbed by an untidy house and need to come out to a clean environment.'

Corporate clients include Bank of Ireland, IBM and Irish

Life. Her pieces are usually large, in the six to ten or twelve foot size range. She also carries out smaller private commissions.

She favours the traditional woven Gobelins technique dating back to the Middle Ages. Working mainly in wools, she uses linen and cotton for detailing, highlighting and lustre, and 'splits' add a three dimensional effect. 'In essence tapestry is a relatively simple technique. It's the manipulation of fibres, imagery and artistry that makes it unique to you.'

She finds her work can be lonely and isolating and while on a commission has little outside contact. To counteract this, Angela has been one of the driving forces behind the formation of a group of contemporary tapestry artists. 'It has made for better contact, but our one constant question is, "Can we take this solitude for the rest of our lives?"'

As her portfolio and reputation have grown, clients approach her because they know her work and style. 'You live with a large tapestry for up to seven months – talking to clients, producing mock-ups, designing, getting the yarns – sometimes they have to be commercially dyed, other times you've to dye them yourself. Then the actual weaving can take about four and a half months of concentrated effort.'

Her work has two sources of inspiration – one which she describes as the 'stone theme' – greys with subtle shades of pinks/blues, atmospheric stones, caves, symbolisms, mysterious communications from the past.

Then there are the bright primary and secondary colours which she develops into gardens and fish pools.

Recent pieces are peopled with female figures and woven words. 'My life feeds into my work and never leaves me. As my work develops creatively, my themes are becoming more universal – almost like letting go of one self to become two selves.'

Part III

Further Facts

Useful Addresses

When you're in business, whether you're operating from home or from a multinational corporation, it's vital to keep in touch with who's who and what's happening where, when, how and why. The following companies, listed in alphabetical order, are useful sources of information:

Allied Irish Bank, Enterprise Development Bureau,
Bankcentre, Ballsbridge, Dublin 4
Tel: (01) 660 0311
Information on range of bank services available to start up businesses; seminars in various locations; 'Help Desk', etc.

Bank of Ireland, Enterprise Support Unit
Head Office, Lower Baggot Street, Dublin 2
Tel: (01) 661 5933
Deals with both start ups and existing businesses at second stage of development.

An Bord Tráchtála (Irish Trade Board)
Merrion Hall, Strand Road, Sandymount, Dublin 4
Tel: (01) 269 5011
(24 overseas offices)
Promotion and development of Irish goods for home and export, plus marketing support services.

Bord Fáilte
Baggot Street Bridge, Dublin 2
Tel: (01) 676 5871

Advisory services on tourism related activities.

Bord Iascaigh Mhara (Irish Sea Fisheries Board)
Crofton Road, Dún Laoghaire, County Dublin
Tel: (01) 284 1544
Promotion of home and export markets for Irish fish products, advisory service and training courses for fishermen and fish farmers.

Business Incubator Centre
Ossory Business Park, 26 Ossory Road,
off North Strand Road, Dublin 3
Tel: (01) 836 3994
also
Richmond Complex, North Brunswick Street, Dublin 7
Tel: (01) 805 0252
Private initiative managed by a team of entrepreneurs whose objective is to help small businesses succeed.

Business Innovation Fund
Molyneux House, 67 Bride Street, Dublin 8
Tel: (01) 475 3305
Provides seed capital for pre-start up activities.

CERT
CERT House, Amiens Street, Dublin 1
Tel: (01) 874 2555
Education, training and recruitment for tourism, hotel and catering industries.

Chambers of Commerce of Ireland,
22 Merrion Square, Dublin 2
Tel: (01) 661 2888
The largest business network in the world – fifty-nine affiliated chambers in Ireland, comprising some 8,000 member firms.

Clonakilty Enterprise Board Ltd
Halla an Bhaile, Kent Street, Clonakilty, West Cork
Tel: (023) 33224
Advice at business start up and expansion stages.

County Development Teams
Department of Enterprise and Employment,
Kildare Street, Dublin 2
Tel: (01) 661 4444
Assistance in conjunction with the Forbairt and other sources of finance; information on setting up new businesses and expanding existing businesses; aftercare service to newly established grant-aided industry.

County Enterprise Boards
Department of Enterprise and Employment,
Kildare Street, Dublin 2
Tel: (01) 661 4444
Assistance through grant-aid in the establisment of small-scale economic projects with the primary aims of facilitating job creation and the development of economic infrastructure at local level.

Crafts Council of Ireland
Top Floor Powerscourt Townhouse, South William Street,
Dublin 2
Tel: (01) 679 7368
Advice and assistance on all aspects of the craft industry.

CSO
Central Statistics Office, St Stephen's Green House, Earlsfort
Terrace, Dublin 2
Tel: (01) 676 7531
Publication of statistics. Access to statistical data bank.

East Cork Enterprise Board Ltd
Europa Enterprise Park, Cork Road, Midleton, County Cork
Tel: (021) 613432
*Advice and consultancy services from a network of local
professional business people.*

First Step
Jefferson House, Eglington Road, Dublin 4
Tel: (01) 260 0988
*Provides start up assistance for projects which cannot access
funding or sufficient funding from other sources.*

FÁS
PO Box 456, 27/33 Upper Baggot Street, Dublin 4
Tel: (01) 668 5777
(National training and placement authority)
Provides training and retraining for employment.

Forbairt
Wilton Park House, Wilton Place, Dublin 2
Tel: (01) 660 2244
also
Glasnevin, Dublin 9
Tel: (01) 837 0101
Responsible for development services to wholly or majority Irish-owned companies; comprehensive information services and library facility.

IBEC
86 Lower Baggot Street, Dublin 2
Tel: (01) 660 1011
(Irish Business and Employers Confederation)
Represents member companies and organisations in relations with the government, trade unions and EU institutions on commercial, economic, industrial and employee issues; also advises on industrial relations, management training, pay and conditions, taxation and trade.

IDA Ireland
Wilton Park House, Wilton Place, Dublin 2
Tel: (01) 668 6633
National responsibility for securing new investment from overseas in manufacturing and international service sectors excluding natural resources based companies; and for encouraging existing foreign enterprises in Ireland to expand their businesses.

IMI
Irish Management Institute, Sandyford Road, Dublin 18
Tel: (01) 295 6911
*Management and supervisory training including Business
Development Programme specifically for owner-managers of
small businesses.*

Innovation Centres

Cork
Southwest Business and Technology Centre,
Enterprise Centre, North Mall, Cork
Tel: (021) 295 6911

Dublin
Dublin Business Innovations Centre,
Enterprise Centre, Pearse Street, Dublin 2
Tel: (01) 677 5655

Galway
IMC Innovation and Management Centre,
Hynes Buildings, St Augustine Street, Galway
Tel: (091) 67974/5/6

Limerick
The Innovation Centre,
Enterprise House, Plassey Technology Park, Limerick
Tel: (061) 338177

*Advice and assistance for small and medium sized businesses
in the development of business plans and market research;
training and development programmes; advice on financial
planning and sources of finance; seed capital and specialist
support services for entrepreneurs and innovators.*

IPC
Irish Productivity Centre, 35 Shelbourne Road, Dublin 4
Tel: (01) 668 6244
*Start Your Own Business training programmes, feasibility
studies, research; also consultancy business advice to small
firms; analysis of production, finance, marketing; job
evaluation assessments.*

IQA
Irish Quality Association, Merrion Hall, Strand Road,
Sandymount, Dublin 4
Tel: (01) 269 5255
*Promotion of quality in industry, organisers of the Quality
Mark Scheme, Hygiene Scheme and training courses.*

ISME Business Association,
32 Kildare Street, Dublin 3
Tel: (01) 662 2755
*Representation of owner-managed business to government,
development agencies, etc.*

NMAC
The National Microelectronics Applications Centre,
Plassey Technological Park, Limerick
Tel: (061) 334699
Electronic product and process design, development and consultancy service.

NOW (New Opportunities for Women)
Council for the Status of Women, 32 Upper Fitzwilliam Street,
Dublin 2
Tel: (01) 661 5268
also
Department of Enterprise and Employment,
Davitt House, Adelaide Road, Dublin 2
Tel: (01) 676 5861
Equal opportunities for women in vocational training and employment, advisory and guidance services, development of childcare facilities, etc.

NSAI
National Standards Authority of Ireland,
Glasnevin, Dublin 9
Tel: (01) 837 0101
Specialist service in Irish and international standards and certifications; register of certified Irish Quality Standard; export certification services for Irish products.

Patents Office
45 Merrion Square, Dublin 2
Tel: (01) 661 4144
Responsible for issuing patents for inventions and registration of designs and trademarks.

Project Development Centre
14 Herbert Street, Dublin 2
Tel: (01) 661 1910
Focus on assisting young Irish graduate entrepreneurs in the areas of innovation, product development and enterprise creation.

SFA
Small Firms Association
86 Lower Baggot Street, Dublin 2
Tel: (01) 660 1011
Representation of small firms in dealings with government on price control, merchandise markets, company taxation, state services, etc.

Shannon Free Airport Development Company Ltd
Shannon Town Centre, County Clare
Tel: (061) 361555
Agency responsible for industrial and tourism development in the Shannon region; provision of product and product development support; start up and expansion incentives; incubator business centre and advance factory units; project appraisal, etc.

Spicers Centre for Europe
43–45 Northumberland Road, Ballsbridge, Dublin 4
Tel: (01) 668 8644
EU research and advisory service.

Teagasc
Agriculture and Food Development Authority
Sandymount Avenue, Dublin 4
Tel: (01) 668 8188
Feasibility studies, resource scheduling and project evaluation services for firms involved in the development of new food products and processes.

Telecottages Ireland
Cork Teleworking Centre, 1 Cornmarket Street, Cork
Tel: (021) 270488
An association to support teleworkers, telecentres and telecottages in Ireland; facilitates members to exchange information and ideas and works to develop technical and administrative systems for commercial teleworking. Research projects examine needs, barriers and opportunities.

Údarás Na Gaeltachta
Na Forbacha, Gaillimh
Tel: (091) 92011
Promotion of industry in the Gaeltacht areas; employment grants; financing; share participation; provisions of factories; training grants; recruitment.

West Cork Business Development Unit
The Sutherland Centre, North Street, Skibbereen,
County Cork
Tel: (028) 21011
Incorporated in the West Cork Education Institute for rural Development, network includes a community school, vocational schools and community colleges. Services comprise multimedia flexible learning, product R and D, business advisory service, etc.

Trade Fairs and Exhibitions

These are big business and a growth area with more and more companies and private individuals jumping on the bandwagon. If you're not at the stage of exhibiting yourself, it's well worth your while attending a trade fair relevant to your product/service. They're a source of instant market research, bring you face to face with your competitors and are a shopfront for what's currently happening in your specific market. As well as which they're a real ideas *fest* and a valuable source of contact.

Publications

National, local and community newspapers, magazines, trade publications and industry directories are useful. Remember to keep a keen eye on the advertisements. Many of these publications are available for reference at various libraries throughout the country, including the Business Library, Ilac Centre, Dublin 1.

These are some of the commercial titles available:

Directories

Dublin Business
Dublin Chamber of Commerce Membership and Buyers'
Directory
Food Ireland Directory
Hotel and Catering Review Yearbook
Irish Industrial Estates Directory
Kompass Register of Irish Industry and Commerce
Production Ireland
Thom's Commercial Directory
Ulster Grocer Yearbook

Magazines/Journals

Advertising and Marketing
Irish Marketing Journal (IMJ)

Marketing

Business Management and Finance

Administration Journal

Aspect Premier 2,000 Irish Companies

Business Contact (Magazine of the Dublin Chamber of Commerce)

Business and Finance

Industry and Commerce

Inside Business (Magazine of the Chambers of Commerce of Ireland)

Others

Advanced Manufacturing Technology

Business and Exporting

Euro Update

The Irish Motor Industry

The Irish Publishing Industry

Manufacturing Ireland

Updata

Addresses of People Profiled

Architects
Tony and Geraldine O'Daly, architects
31 Terenure Road East, Dublin 6. Tel: (01) 496 7159

Artists
Anne O'Shea and Maurice Noble
29 Balbriggan Street, Skerries, County Dublin.
Tel: (01) 849 2709

Bird Houses
Simone Stephenson
The Birdhouse Company, Bartra, Harbour Road, Dalkey,
County Dublin. Tel: (01) 280 1936

Cakes
Jill Aston
Cake Craft, 4 Ulverton Close, Dalkey, County Dublin.
Tel: (01) 284 1137

Candles
Ciaran Ganter
Candlewood, 1 Farmhill Park, Dublin 14. Tel: (01) 298 0407

Catering
Maher family, Boyton Catering
47 North Avenue, Mount Merrion, County Dublin.
Tel: (01) 288 2702/288 5774

Computer Work Station
Patrick Quilligan
Design House, 37 Daniel Street, off Clanbrassil Street, Dublin 8.
Tel: (01) 453 9855

Electronic Shopping Mall
Tony O'Connell
Channel-One, 35 Parliament Street, Dublin 2.
Tel: (01) 679 0004; mobile: (088) 502136

Health Centre
Dhara Kelly and Emer Gaffney
Cloona Health Centre, Westport, County Mayo.
Tel: (098) 25251

Marketing
Marie Cooney
Tipperary Natural Mineral Water Company,
15 Cherry Orchard Estate, Dublin 10.
Tel: (01) 626 9787

Ostrich Farming
Brian Purcell
Royal County Farm, Clonee, County Meath. Tel: (01) 825 5122

Pottery
Dave Dain
Poulavone, Kilsheelin, Clonmel, County Tipperary.
Tel: (051) 646120

Tapestries
Anglea Forte
78 Kincora Road, Clontarf, Dublin 3. Tel: (01) 833 9881

Teddy Bears
Joan Hanna
Craft T-Bear, Mount Windsor, Farnahoe, Innishannon, County
Cork. Tel: (021) 775470

Teleworking
Regina McGarrigle
Mayo Editorial Services, Ballynew, Castlebar, County Mayo.
Tel: (094) 23334

Tourism
Gubbins family
Rent-an-Irish Cottage Ltd, 85 O'Connell Street, Limerick.
Tel: (061) 314667

Bibliography and Further Reading

Cannon, Tom (ed.), *How to Get Ahead in Business.* London: Virgin Books, 1993.

Foley, Edel, *Irish Business Management.* Dublin: Gill and Macmillan, 1989.

Jones, Maxine, *Successful Irish Business Women.* Cork: Mercier Press, 1992.

Hayden, Fionnuala, *Whose Housework is it Anyway?* Dublin: Marino Books, 1995.

McMahon, Denis, *On Line to Success.* Dublin: Poolbeg, 1993.

O'Kane, Brian, *Starting a Business in Ireland.* Dublin: Oak Tree Press, 1993.

Rudinger, Edith (ed.), *Starting Your Own Business.* London: Consumers' Association, 1983.

Scott, David, A., *Psychology and the World of Work.* London: Macmillan Press, 1994.

Sproxton, Edel, *Starting and Running a Small Business.* Cornwall: United Writers, 1979.

Temple, Christopher, *Working from Home.* Oxford: Madison Square, 1993.

Acknowledgements

Thanks to:

Those who agreed to be profiled and identified
Those who chose to remain anonymous but who provided
valuable information

Thanks also to:

Allied Irish Bank
Bank of Ireland
W. J. Arundel, CDVEC
Hilary Kennedy, CLÉ
Sean O'Farrell, Crafts Council
The Credit Union
Mary McCarthy, FÁS
Colm O'Doherty, First Step
Roderick Long, Inter Company Comparisons Limited (ICC)
Nessa Coonan, IDA
Rory Hearne, Kate Cowhig International Recruitment
Tony Moore, Consulting Engineer
Noeleen Kelly, Norwich Union
Margaret Whelan, The Project Development Centre
Evelyn Barrett, Revenue Commissioners
Lillie Toner, Telecom Éireann
Imogen Bertin, Telecottages Ireland